The Macmillan Colour Library

Insects

Ralph Whitlock

MACMILLAN CHILDREN'S BOOKS
LONDON

Contents

Introduction 4

Millions of Insects
Insects Families 6
Parts of an Insect 8
Insect Reproduction 10
An Insect's Development 12

The Life of Insects
Time to Sleep 14
Hungry Larvae 16
Adult Insects 18
Predatory Insects 20

Insect Societies and Communities
Bees and Wasps 22
Ants and Termites 24
Locusts and Grasshoppers 26
Living in Crowds 28

Insects and Colours
Butterflies and Moths 30
Camouflage 32
Mimicry and Warning Colours 34
Dragonflies, Beetles and Others 36

Strange and Specialized Insects
Giants and Monsters 38
Insects with Strange Homes 40
Enemies of Man 42
Aquatic Insects 44

Large Mexican Grasshopper 46

Observing Insects and Glossary 48

Index 49

Right: This hairy ugly nymph will one day emerge as a lovely Golden-ringed dragonfly, which is one of the largest of the dragonflies. The adult gets its name from the black and golden rings around its body, but the nymph is dull brown all over.

Editor: Miranda Smith
Designer: Julian Holland
Picture researcher: Stella Martin

Photo credits:
Heather Angel/Biofotos 6 below left, 8, 9 below, 15 below left, 16, 16-17 above, 17 above, 18 above, 19 above left, 21, 22 below, 23 above, 27 above, 29 right, 33 above, 34 above and below, 36 above, 39 below, 40-41 below, 41 above, 42, 44 above and below right, 45; Aquila Photographics 23 below; Sdeuard C. Bisserot 16-17 below; Michael Chinery 37 above left, 41 below; Bruce Coleman 10-11, 28-29; Food and Agricultural Organization 26 above; Ian Griffiths 24; Frank W. Lane 7 below, 36 below; A.E. Pearce 35 below; Natural History Photographic Agency 2-3. 4-5, 6-7, 7 above, 10 above, 11 above and below, 12-13, 14 above and below, 15 above and below right, 17 below, 19 above right and below, 20 above, 22 above, 24-25 above and below, 26 below, 27 below, 28, 30-31 above, 32, 32-33 above and below, 33 below, 35 above, 37 above right and below, 38 above, 40 below, 40-41 above, 42-43, 43 above and below; Natural Science Photos 6 below right; Premaphotos Wildlife 20 below left, 25 above, 29 left, 30, 30-31 below, 31 above and below, 38 below, 46-47; Spectrum Colour Library 25 below, 44 below left; ZEFA 9 above, 10 below, 18 below, 20 below right, 39 above, 48.

Cover picture: Natural History Photographic Agency
Endpaper artwork: Nicholas Hall

First published in 1983 by
Macmillan Children's Books
a division of Macmillan Publishers Limited
4 Little Essex Street, London WC2R 3LF
and Basingstoke
Associated companies throughout the world

ISBN 0 333 34074 4

Printed in Hong Kong

Front cover: The male Luna moth has enormous feathered antennae. It is one of the world's largest moths.
Right: The Lycid beetle, found in South Africa, has strange flattened wing-cases and feeds on plant-tissues.

Introduction

Insects are the record-breakers of the animal world. This is not surprising, as there are so many of them. There are probably more than one million different sorts of insects in the world. And there are enormous numbers of almost every sort. A gigantic swarm of locusts once seen flying over the Red Sea was estimated to cover 5,000 square kilometres. There were approximately 250,000 million insects in that swarm, and that was of one species only.

The top 22 centimetres of soil in temperate countries often contains as many as 5,000 tiny insects called springtails. There are springtails almost everywhere. They have been found in the extreme cold of Antarctica, only 1,400 kilometres from the South Pole.

Some insects can do marvellous things. Male Emperor moths can detect the scent of a female more than nine kilometres away. Bees and some moths and other insects can see ultra-violet light, which is invisible to us. A flea can jump 130 times its own height!

A queen termite can lay 30 eggs a minute and continue doing so for nearly 50 years. Mayflies live for only a few hours and have no mouth parts because they never need to eat. Some termites regulate the ventilation of their nests by an elaborate system of airducts; they heat their nests by growing heat-producing fungi. Some ants, too, cultivate fungi as food. Other ants sew leaves together with silk threads to form their nests. Others capture slave ants to do their work for them. Wasps make paper for nest-building by mixing wood pulp with their saliva. The caterpillars of the Large White butterfly can only complete their growth and become chrysalids if they are carried into an ants' nest by the ants.

Insects can be dangerous as well. They often spread disease – for example, large areas of Africa are made uninhabitable by the tsetse fly because it carries sleeping sickness. In other places, beetles and their larvae eat vast quantities of grain which would otherwise be used to feed human beings.

Right: The Hawker dragonfly is common in Europe and in the Mediterranean countries. It has shiny colours of green, blue, yellow and brown, with wide transparent wings.

Insect Families

There are about one million different kinds of insects in the world. Scientists divide them into 29 groups (or orders). On these pages you will see pictures of five of these groups.

Some are social insects, like the honey bee. Social insects live in groups, or colonies, and help each other. Some like the grasshopper, belong to warm climates or summer sunshine. Some are more common, everyday creatures, like the fly and the flea. Some are very beautiful, like the dragonfly and the butterfly.

Bees feed on nectar from flowers and take some to their hives for their young. During the summer months, they also store honey, made from nectar, for winter food. From the flowers they also collect pollen for making cells in their hives. Some of the cells contain bee larvae, and some are store-rooms for honey.

Butterflies, too, sip nectar, but do not store it or care for their young. Dragonflies eat other insects, catching them on the wing, but grasshoppers feed mostly on grass. Fleas suck blood from animals. Flies eat decaying animal matter and are Nature's dustmen. But they are also carriers of disease germs.

This honey-bee is collecting nectar from willowherb flowers. It will take the nectar back to the hive and store it as honey for the larvae to eat and also as food for the winter. At the same time, it collects pollen for making the wax cells in which the honey is stored and where the larvae live. When the bee enters the next flower, some of the pollen rubs off and so fertilizes the flower. Bees are

Most grasshoppers live in hot countries or are seen only in summer. They sing only when the temperature is high. They have no real voice, but sing by scraping one leg against another or against some other part of their bodies. They are usually harmless insects, eating leaves and grasses. But locusts, which are a kind of grasshopper, sometimes are so numerous that they eat every living plant in fields and gardens over a wide area.

This Blow-fly seems to be feeding on a slice of bread and honey. In fact, it is sucking up only the honey. It cannot eat solid food but can suck up the juices of decaying flesh. Blow-flies are a danger to health because they spread germs. Before settling on our food they may have been walking on the droppings of some animal, or exploring somebody's dustbin. They also lay their eggs on meat, and the larvae feed on the meat.

social insects and live in colonies or swarms. 50,000 bees or more may live in one hive. By storing honey in summer, the whole swarm can stay alive through the winter.

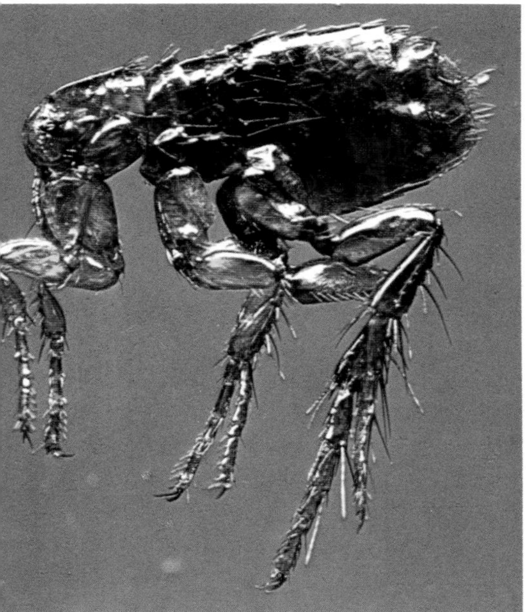

The flea also spreads disease germs as it moves from one animal to another. It lives by sucking blood, and the germs enter the bodies of the victims through the punctures it makes. When fleas were very common, they spread many terrible epidemics. One was the Black Death, which killed 25 million people in Europe in the Middle Ages.

Fleas move by leaping as well as by crawling. A flea can jump 130 times its own height. The largest flea in the world measures four millimetres.

This magnificent dragonfly lives in southern Florida, in the United States. Dragonflies are usually found by rivers, lakes and other wet places or in woods. They spend their early lives under water as nymphs. Both the nymphs and the mature insects are carnivorous. They feed on other insects.

Butterflies, including this lovely Paradise Swallowtail which lives in the tropics, are among the most beautiful of insects. Often their colours are the same as the brightly-coloured flowers which they visit to sip nectar. The colours help to camouflage them.

Parts of an Insect

An insect's body seems to be inside-out when compared to a mammal's. Its skeleton is on the outside. The skeleton consists of a thin, hard coat of armour, known as 'chitin'. Once this armour has set hard it cannot expand, so when the insect grows, it has to split open its body-shell, shed it and grow another. This process is known as 'moulting'.

Insects have no lungs, but breathe through tiny holes, known as 'spiracles', in the sides of their bodies. Oxygen penetrates into their bodies very slowly, along canals called 'tracheae'. This system will work only in creatures which have small bodies, so insects are not very large. All adult insects, even those which live in water, breathe air, though many larvae extract what oxygen they need from water.

As much as 75 per cent of the weight of an insect may consist of blood, but the blood does not carry oxygen, as in mammals. Instead, it is employed chiefly in carrying away waste material. When a winged insect, such as a butterfly or locust, emerges from the chrysalis stage, it hangs from a stem or leaf while its body pumps blood into the limp, crumpled wings. These soon expand and harden, and the blood is then withdrawn.

The mouth parts of insects vary greatly, according to the food which the insect eats. Caterpillars usually have jaws like scissors with serrated edges, for cutting and chewing plant tissues. Butterflies have long, slender tongues, often rolled in a coil, which are designed to penetrate trumpet-shaped flowers and sip the nectar. Some flies have sharp, dagger-like mouth-parts for piercing skin and sucking blood. Some of them, when doing so, inject a local anaesthetic so that the victim does not know he is being attacked.

Like many other insects, the Horse-fly, or Deer-fly, has huge, multiple eyes. Each eye has many lenses packed close together. They enable the fly to see things above, below, behind and around it, which is why it is extremely difficult to hit such flies. It is not known what it is like to see through multiple eyes, but the world probably appears as a rather blurred mosaic pattern. When some of the lenses are in focus, some of the others are bound to be out of focus

Below: An insect's body is divided into three main parts – the head, the thorax and the abdomen. The six legs are attached to the thorax. The head contains the brain and some of the sense organs. Some of the organs are arranged differently from ours. For instance, some grasshoppers have ears in their legs.

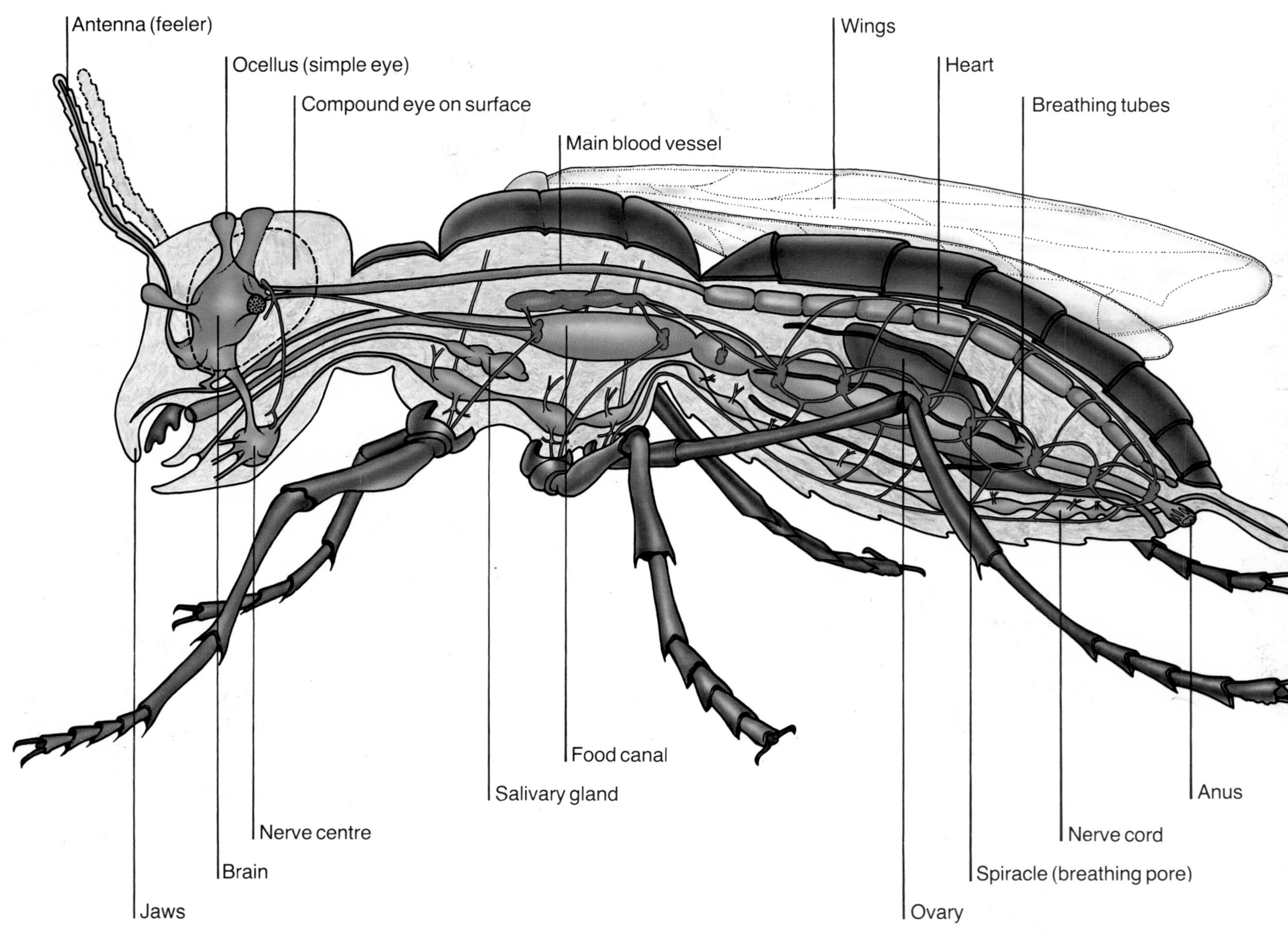

The male Cockchafer, which is a kind of beetle, has curious fan-shaped antennae. These are very sensitive to scent and enable it to find its mate over long distances. A big, handsome insect, the Cockchafer comes out at twilight, humming in flight and sometimes crashing against lighted windows. It does damage by eating leaves and flowers.

Butterflies have wings covered with tiny, coloured scales, so small that they rub off like powder when they are touched. The scales are of different shapes, but each has a stalk which fits into a socket on the frame of the wing. They are arranged in overlapping rows, all anchored to slope away from the front edge of the wing, thus helping the air to flow over the wing surface.

Insects are very adaptable. They can adjust themselves to heat and cold, to salt deserts and hot springs – in fact, to almost every environment on earth, except sea-water. No insects live in the deep sea, though many are found on shores which are covered with water at high tide. There is even one insect, a small fly, whose larvae live only in waste oil around oil-wells. Insects are known to eat such unlikely substances as boot polish, sandpaper, carpets, books, tobacco and poisonous fungi, as well as the internal organs of living creatures. Some of the insects do enormous damage, and in time they become immune to the poisonous chemicals with which we try to control them.

One of the most effective methods of controlling insect pests, however, is to set other insects to prey on them. Ladybirds, for example, eat greenflies, which are often a pest on rose-bushes. Tiny wasps, known as Chalcid wasps, are used to control woolly aphids and white-flies. Insects can help in fighting plant pests, too. So insect appetites can be made to work for men as well as against them.

Insect Reproduction

Most insects, though not all, pass through four stages during their lives. They begin inside an egg, from which a larva hatches. The larva spends most of its time eating and growing. When it has grown to its full size, it changes into a pupa or chrysalis. Later, the adult insect (imago) emerges from the pupa.

The egg and pupa stages are very useful to insects, because in these forms they can stand long periods of bad weather. As eggs or pupae some insects can be frozen without coming to any harm. And, because they are frozen, they do not need to feed.

The lovely Luna moth is sitting on a chrysalis from which it has just emerged. The chrysalis is wrapped in silk and so is known as a cocoon. The silk is spun by the caterpillar when it is ready to turn into a chrysalis. The caterpillar of the Silk moth spins nearly one kilometre of silk to make its cocoon.

The larva of the Wood-wasp needs no protection, because it lives inside a tree-trunk, eating the wood. When it turns into a chrysalis (or pupa) it stays safely in its tunnel until the time comes for it to emerge. Then the newly-hatched wasp bites its way out.

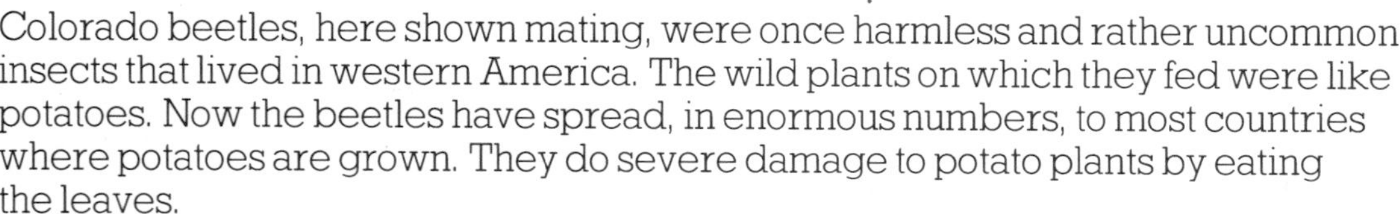

Colorado beetles, here shown mating, were once harmless and rather uncommon insects that lived in western America. The wild plants on which they fed were like potatoes. Now the beetles have spread, in enormous numbers, to most countries where potatoes are grown. They do severe damage to potato plants by eating the leaves.

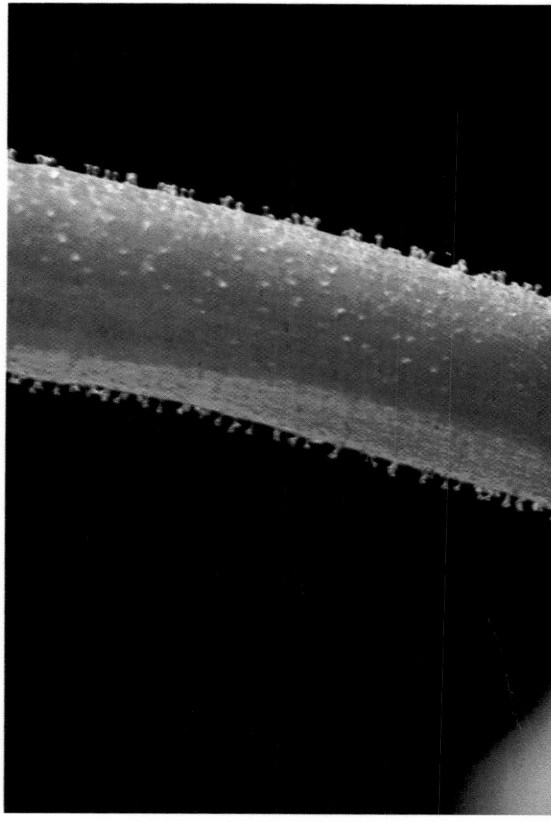

During summer months, several generations of female aphids produce living young without ever having to look for a mate. They multiply so quickly that they often become great

Left: A male Empid-fly has to catch a small insect and offer it to the female before he can mate. Mating can begin when she starts to eat it. Sometimes he tries to deceive the female by offering a silk-wrapped parcel of rubbish, or even an empty package. By the time the female has finished unwrapping the parcel the male is ready to fly away!

Empid-flies are very common. Swarms of them can often be seen dancing over water. We usually call them gnats.

Above: This Luna moth is sitting on the cocoon from which it has just emerged. The enormous feathered antennae show that it is a male moth. They are extremely sensitive to scent, and are used by the male to find a female, often over great distances. When the male is downwind from the female he can sometimes locate her at a distance of up to eight kilometres.

The Luna or Moon moth has a wing-span of up to 12 centimetres. It is found in India, while a similar moth lives in North America.

Most adult insects mate, but some manage differently. In the picture below centre, an aphid is giving birth to a living young one. This young aphid is female and will produce many more living young without ever mating. More and more aphids are born in this way, until in late summer the last generation consists of both males and females, which mate in the normal way. The eggs laid by the female then remain as eggs all the winter. When spring comes, all the aphids that hatch from them are females which do not need to mate. This strange process is known as parthenogenesis.

Not many insects care for their young. Bees, wasps, ants and termites are exceptions. Most female insects, however, take care to lay their eggs near a food supply for the larvae, even when they themselves do not eat the same sort of food.

Mayflies do not feed at all, but lay their eggs in the water where their larvae have to live. Sometimes they even crawl into the water to lay their eggs on underwater plants. Scarab beetles take a lot of care in the preparation of balls of dung, in the centre of which the female lays an egg. The larva feeds on the dung.

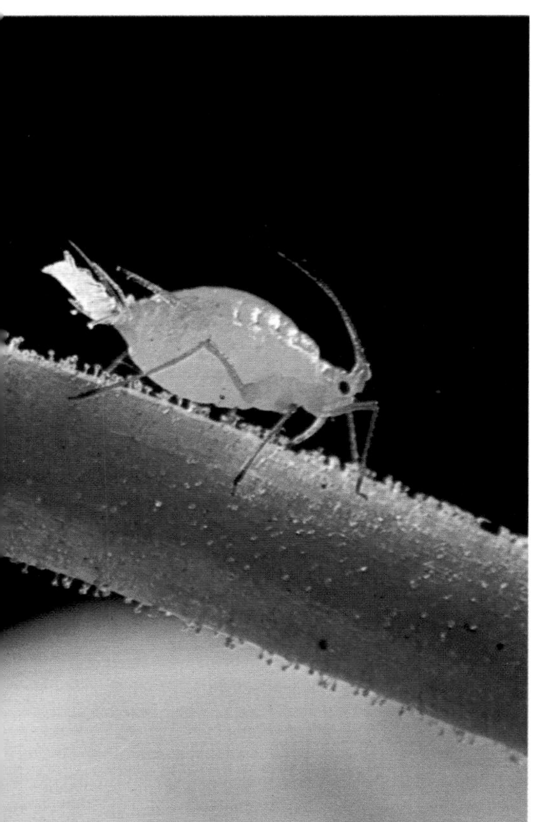

pests, doing much damage by sucking the juices from plants. A single aphid can produce as many as 1,300 descendants in a fortnight. Some aphids in each generation have wings.

What appears to be the sting of this Wood wasp is really an ovipositor, designed for boring holes and laying eggs in hard wood. The female lays only one egg in each hole. On her legs she often carries the spores of certain fungi or moulds. When these grow in the hole they provide food for the larvae. The larvae also feed on the wood. The Wood wasp has no sting and so cannot harm us.

Peacock butterflies go through the four stages of insect life during one spring and summer. They lay their eggs in spring. When the caterpillars emerge in summer they eat and grow as fast as they can. While they are growing they are in great danger of being snapped up by birds. The black spines help to protect them. When a caterpillar is nearly fully grown, it spins a little pad of silk and attaches it to the leaf or stem of a plant. From this it hangs and turns into a chrysalis. As it matches the plant in colour, it is well camouflaged. Other caterpillars bind themselves to a stalk or twig with strands of silk when they pupate. Caterpillars of some butterflies and moths burrow underground when they are ready to form chrysalids. Their chrysalids are usually dark brown. This means that they match the soil and so are well camouflaged.

Peacock butterflies emerge in late summer and fly from flower to flower. When cold weather comes, they creep into hollow trees, sheds or empty rooms and hibernate. In spring they wake up and fly away, searching for places to lay their eggs. The whole process then repeats itself.

Dragonflies spend far longer than butterflies in the early stages of their lives. The eggs are laid in summer and soon hatch. But the nymph stage, which comes next, may last for several years. The nymphs, which live under water, do not change into chrysalids. Instead, they change their skins as they grow, many of them doing so as many as ten or fifteen times. Dragonfly nymphs are among the fiercest creatures living in ponds and rivers. They feed on other insects and crustaceans and even on tadpoles and small fish. When they are ready to moult for the last time, they crawl up a plant stem. The skin splits, and a dragonfly emerges.

Dragonflies have no larva and chrysalis stages. Instead, they have a form called the nymph, which combines the two. This stage of their life, which is spent in water, lasts from one to five years.

The life of a Peacock butterfly

Above: When the caterpillar is ready to pupate (become a chrysalis), it spins a little pad of silk. It attaches this pad to a leaf or stem and hangs from it. This one is well camouflaged.

Right: After a few weeks, the beautiful Peacock butterfly emerges from the chrysalis and spreads its wings.

Above: When the Peacock butterfly caterpillars grow bigger they move about the nettle plant and feed singly. This caterpillar is nearly fully grown.

Left: The Peacock butterfly lays its eggs on the leaves of a nettle plant. When the caterpillars first hatch they will feed together in a group.

4

It is easy to recognize a bird's egg. It is always oval. Insect eggs are of all shapes, and, unlike birds' eggs, they are not laid in nests. The pictures on this spread show some examples. The Blow-fly eggs are so firmly attached to the hairs of the animal that it is very difficult for it to scratch or rub them off. Some mosquito eggs are stuck together in batches and float on water, like rafts. Some Plant-bugs have eggs with little lids, which the larvae push open when they are ready to come out.

For an insect, becoming a pupa is something like returning to the egg stage. As larvae, most insects have eyes and other senses, and these give them information about their surroundings. As a pupa, the insect is enclosed in a hard case, without external sense organs. Inside the shell, profound changes take place. The materials of the larva's body are recycled to form the head, thorax, abdomen, wings, legs, eyes and other organs of the perfect insect.

Most insects spend only a short time in the egg stage, except when the eggs are laid in late summer or autumn and have to survive the winter. The pupa stage usually lasts much longer. In countries with a fairly long winter it is normal for butterflies and moths to spend the winter as chrysalids.

When the caterpillars of the South African Emperor moth hatch from their white oval eggs they are little greenish caterpillars. You can see the empty egg-shells in the picture. You can also see the black heads of the larvae in the eggs which have not yet hatched.

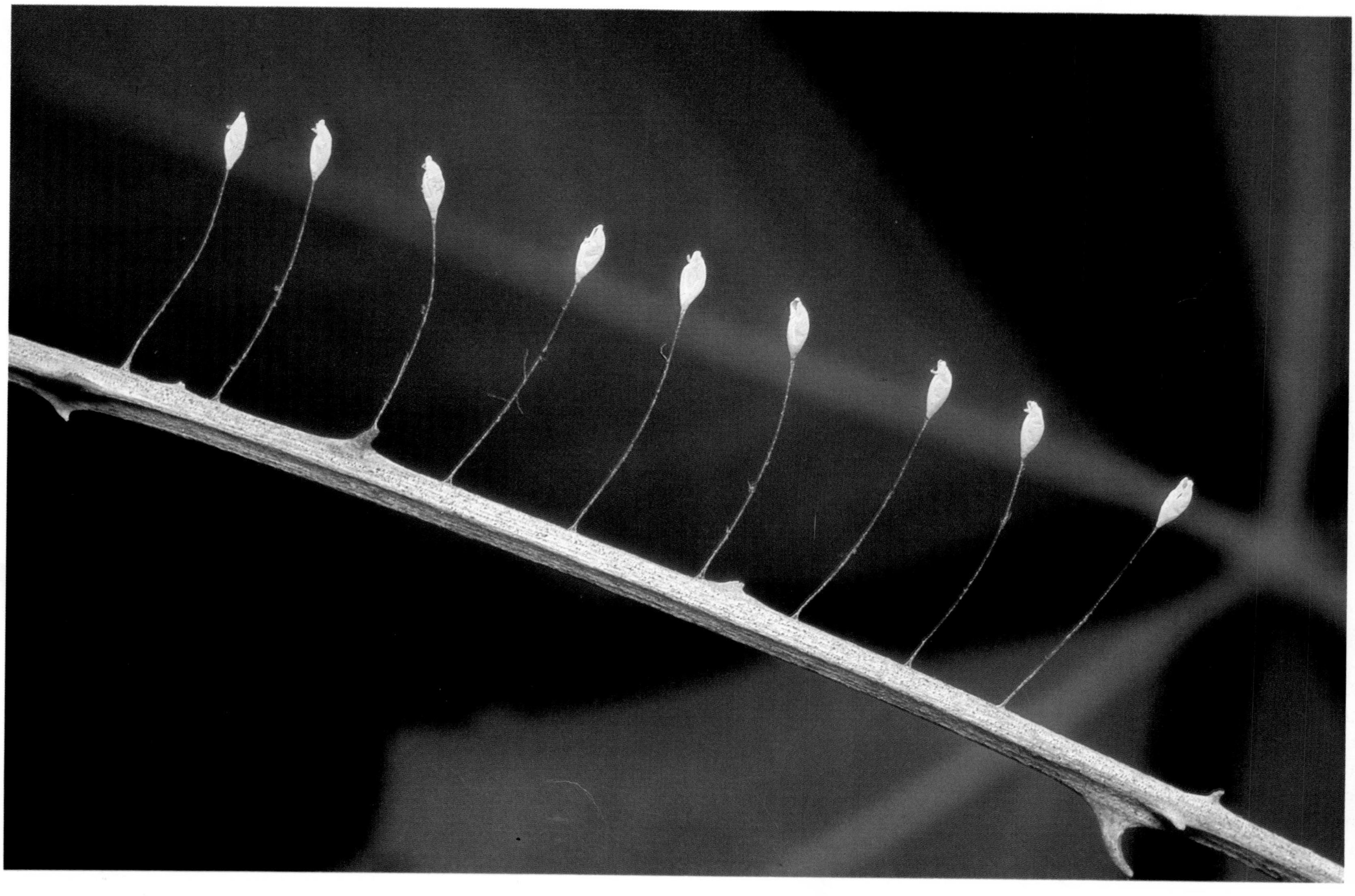

Left: The Blow-fly lays its eggs on dead animals, animal waste or meat. It sometimes lays them on live animals as well. The eggs in this picture are attached to the hairs of a cow. When the larvae emerge, they have a plentiful food-supply around them. The lovely, glittering greenbottle fly, which is a kind of blowfly, likes to lay its eggs on the wool of sheep. The larvae burrow into the living flesh.

In houses, Blow-flies are a pest because they try to lay their eggs on meat, which may become contaminated with maggots (the larvae of the Blow-fly). The larvae are strange creatures. They are fat, white sausage-like maggots, large at one end and tapering at the other. Their head is at the narrow end, but they breathe through pores (spiracles) at the broad end.

Above: Although the caterpillar of the Privet Hawk-moth is bright green with mauve and white stripes, the chrysalis is dark reddish-brown. This means that it matches the soil in which it buries itself. The caterpillars, which are large and plump, are fully grown in autumn. They crawl down to the base of their food plant, bury themselves for winter, and emerge the following summer.

Left: Each of the eggs of the Lacewing is laid at the tip of a long stalk. The insect lays a drop of sticky fluid on the stalk and pulls it into a fine thread. This hardens quickly, and the fly then lays an egg at the tip. Ants and other insects crawling along the stem notice only the stalks and miss the eggs which they might otherwise eat. Lacewing larvae are carnivorous. They catch other small insects, especially aphids, and suck out their juices.

A Monarch butterfly emerges from a chrysalis which hangs from a stalk. Its wings have not yet unfolded. Fluid is pumped into the veins which unfolds the wings. They are still soft at first and will take about an hour to harden sufficiently.

Hungry Larvae

Most of the insects that are regarded as enemies by men are most troublesome in the larva stage. Insect eggs and pupae do not eat; nor do some adult insects. Others, like butterflies only sip nectar from flowers and do no harm. But insect larvae eat most of the time. That is what larvae are for. They have to grow large enough to provide enough material to make the adult insect inside the chrysalis case later.

Most female insects which lay the eggs usually take a lot of trouble to place them near a food supply for the larvae when they hatch. Butterflies lay their eggs on the right food-plant. The female butterfly has organs on her feet, something like the taste-buds on our tongues. These enable her to 'sense' whether the plant is right. Some caterpillars can eat only one sort of plant, and if the butterfly was to make a mistake they would starve.

Blow-flies lay their eggs on meat; greenbottle flies lay theirs on the flesh of living animals, especially sheep. The larvae, which are white maggots, eat into the flesh. Ichneumon flies and some wasps lay their eggs inside the bodies of caterpillars or spiders, and the unfortunate victims are eaten alive by the larvae. When Sexton beetles find a small dead animal, such as a mouse or mole, they start to bury it. They do this by digging away the soil under it, so that the carcase sinks into the ground. When the animal is buried, the female beetle lays her eggs in a tunnel nearby. She herself feeds the larvae with liquids she collects from the decaying corpse.

Although larvae do much damage by eating food plants or animals valuable to human beings, they do even more by spreading disease. Some pass on diseases to people, but others pass them to animals and plants. For example, the larvae of the Elm-bark beetle carry the germs of deadly Dutch elm disease.

The Pale Tussock moth caterpillar has tufts of golden-coloured hairs, like those of a toothbrush, on its back. It also has a reddish brown tuft for a tail. Then there is a light covering of other hairs. All the hairs are sensitive when touched and so help to protect the caterpillar against birds. When a bird tries to take hold of a

The Elm-bark beetle lays its eggs between the bark and the wood of the elm tree trunk. The female beetle herself makes the first tunnel, in which mating takes place. Here, she also lays her eggs. When the larvae hatch, each makes a tunnel at right angles to the first one. They eat the bark and wood as they go. They also carry disease germs that attack the tree.

When Blow-fly larvae are fully grown, their outer skin becomes dark brown. It also becomes so hard that when the fly is ready to emerge, it has to force its way out. It does this by inflating a

caterpillar, the hairs move and frighten the bird. Also, the hairs have barbed tips which break off and stick in the bird's mouth, irritating it. The hairs are later spun into the cocoons.

The caterpillars of the Small Ermine moth know how to protect themselves. They do this by feeding together in a colony. They surround themselves by a web. Sometimes several colonies, made up from eggs laid by several females, are found in the same hedge. The caterpillars' favourite food is the spindle-tree and they will strip the tree of its leaves.

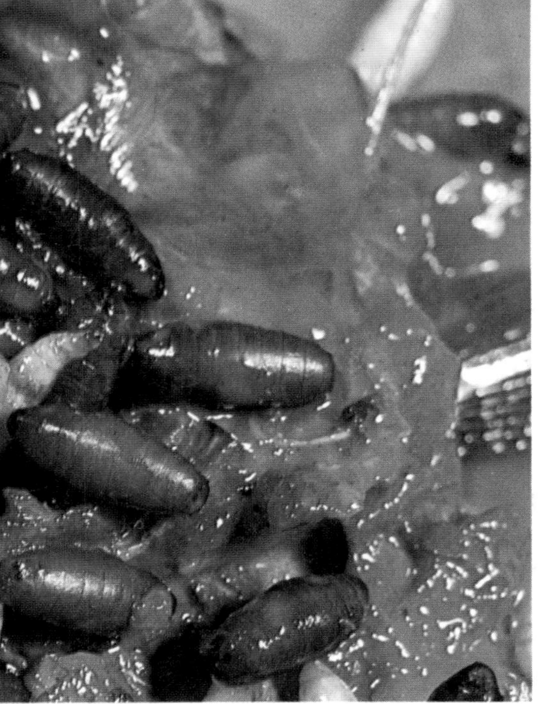

special bladder which splits the skin. In the picture, some of the pupae have developed their hard shells, while others are still creamy-white in colour and their shells are softer.

The round, hard, marble-like galls on oak twigs are produced by the larvae of the Gall wasp, which feeds inside the twig. This causes the gall to form around it. There is only one larva in each gall. The galls are first green but then turn brown in autumn, when the adult wasp eats its way out, making the round holes shown in the picture.

In the larva stage, insects have to eat and grow as fast as possible. In the adult stage, their chief purpose is to breed, so that there will be more insects of the same sort next year.

Many insects have brightly-coloured bodies. The colours act as a warning and protect them against predators; especially birds. For example, Soldier-beetles are bright red. A young bird, catching sight of such an attractive insect, will try to eat it but will find it has a most unpleasant taste. From that moment, all bright red insects will be safe from that bird. The bodies of other insects contain poisons which make the birds avoid them. The Monarch butterfly obtains its poisons from its food-plant. Its bright colours warn birds to leave it alone.

Aphids are helped by the fact that there are huge numbers of them. Even if enemies eat thousands of them, there are still plenty left to breed. Aphids with wings fly to different plants and increase quickly in number there. The descendants of a single aphid which began laying eggs in spring could number many millions by the end of summer, if they all survived.

Soldier-beetles are so called because they are dressed in red, like some soldiers used to be. The colour is a warning to predators that they are not good to eat. As a result they do not bother to hide – instead they 'advertise' their colours. The red of the beetles in this picture stands out clearly against the yellow of the plant.

Above: A honey-bee looks for nectar in a sage flower. The shape of the flower means that the bee has to push hard to enter it. The pollen then rubs off on to the bee's back. In the picture we can see the tiny yellow grains of pollen clinging to the bee's hairs. They are then carried to other flowers to fertilize them. The nectar is at the base of the flower and the bee needs a very long tongue to reach it.

Right: Monarch butterflies are great travellers. This Monarch lives in Africa, but American Monarchs make tremendous journeys – sometimes 130 kilometres a day without stopping. They have strong wings, which measure up to 85 millimetres across. They migrate northwards in spring in such large numbers that tourists make special journeys to see them passing.

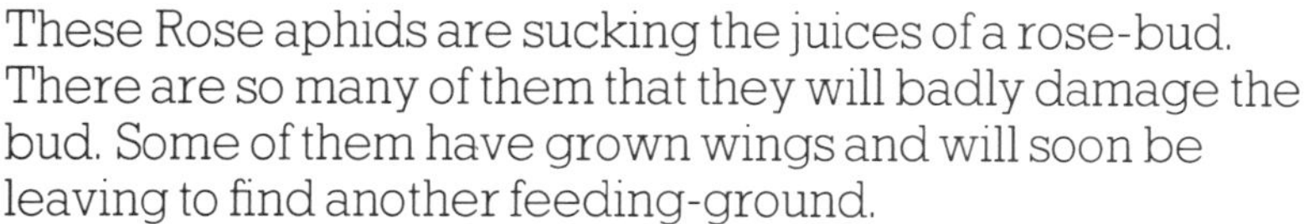

These Rose aphids are sucking the juices of a rose-bud. There are so many of them that they will badly damage the bud. Some of them have grown wings and will soon be leaving to find another feeding-ground.

When Mayflies emerge as adult insects, most of them live for only a day. Some live only a few hours. Their lives are so short that they have no need to eat and so they have no mouth-parts. They simply dance in the sunshine, mate and die.

May-flies emerge in enormous numbers on a single day in spring. There are so many of them, dancing in the sunlight by streams and ponds, that it is easy for them to find mates. That is all they have to do, so they have no need to eat. They mate and, when the eggs are laid, they die.

There are three kinds of bee in the hive of the honey-bees. The most important bee in the hive is the queen bee. Without her, the colony would die. It is she who lays all the eggs from which the other bees hatch. There can be only one queen bee in a hive. If another appears, the two fight to the death.

Once during the summer a new queen is hatched. She escapes quickly from the hive and flies high into the air. At the same time some drones, which are males, are also hatched. They follow the queen, and one meets and mates with her. Then it falls to the ground, dying. The queen then flies away with many of them to find a new hive or site for a nest.

Most honey-bees are workers. They are really females which cannot breed but which have to feed and care for the bee larvae. It is they who collect the nectar and pollen from the flowers.

Predatory Insects

Many insects prey on other insects. Pictures on these pages show a Robber-fly killing a bee, ladybirds eating aphids and a Praying Mantis which has captured a cricket. The Robber-fly has probably lain in ambush for the bee and pounced on it when it came to feed at a flower. But it may have caught the bee in flight.

Ladybirds eat enormous numbers of aphids and so are very useful. Their larvae, which are fierce-looking creatures, mauve and orange in colour, also feed on aphids. The numbers of ladybirds greatly increase in summers when aphids are especially numerous.

Mantids are found mostly in tropical countries, where some of them grow to a length of 20 centimetres. They are expert in camouflage, lying in wait among flowers or leaves until their prey ventures within reach. Then they strike very quickly. Some of the bigger ones attack small birds, reptiles and mammals as well as insects, and the female often eats the male after they have mated.

Among the fiercest hunters are the Ground-beetles, which we find under stones in the garden. Most of them can run very fast and so overtake their prey. Dragonflies, both as nymphs and adult insects, also prey on other insects.

Ladybirds are the gardener's friends. They are really beetles. Both the adult beetles and the larvae feed on the aphids, which do much harm by sucking plant juices. Under their brightly-coloured wing-cases they have gauzy wings and can fly quite well.

This Robber-fly, which is a big, hairy insect, has captured a honey-bee and is sucking its blood. It stabbed its victim with its sharp beak or proboscis, and the unfortunate bee was killed instantly. Some Robber-flies catch their prey in flight; others lie in ambush and pounce on their victims. They are bold and aggressive, attacking insects much larger than themselves. But they are quite harmless to human beings.

Horse-flies are large insects, some having a wing-spread of five centimetres. The females attack cattle, horses and humans, piercing the skin with their sharp mouth-parts and then sucking the blood. Their bite is often quite painful. Some Horse-flies, especially in the tropics, infect their victims with the germs of dangerous diseases. Male Horse-flies feed on nectar in flowers and are quite harmless. Horse-flies fly in summer, and many of them have very beautiful, golden-green eyes. The colours, however, fade quickly after death.

The Praying Mantis gets its name because it looks as if it is praying. Actually, it is holding up its legs in readiness to pounce on its prey. The Mantis in the picture has just caught a cricket and is eating it. Although mantids can fly, they spend most of their time lying in wait to catch other insects. They use many disguises, some of them resembling flowers or twigs. This one looks like the spikes of the gorse-bush on which it is sitting.

Inside a bee-hive we see so many bees, all looking exactly alike, running around and crawling over each other. They are, in fact, taking care of the young bees.

In the picture on the right, you can see some of the larvae. They are pearly-white grubs, curled up in cells. Some of the bees are building new cells, with wax made from pollen collected from flowers. Others are filling the cells with honey, for future use. Some are feeding the bee larvae; some are feeding other workers whose duties keep them in the hive; some will be feeding the queen. The queen herself is wandering about the hive, laying eggs in empty cells.

A strong colony of hive-bees will consist of 50,000 bees or more. As the numbers increase in early summer, some of the workers prepare to leave the hive, to form a new colony. To do so they must have another queen, which they can produce to order. All the bee larvae are fed at first on a protein-rich substance called 'royal jelly', which the worker bees make from nectar. After three days, most of the larvae have their diet changed to a mixture of nectar and pollen, but the larvae destined to be queens are still fed on the royal jelly.

The worker bees in this picture are always busy. When they are first hatched they stay in the hive. There, they clean and repair cells and feed the young bees. Later, they leave the hive to gather nectar from flowers. As many as 50,000 bees may live in one hive.

Three kinds of bee live in a hive. They are the queen, which lays all the eggs; the drones, which are males; and the workers, which do all the work in and outside the hive. The worker bees are really female, though they do not mate or lay eggs.

This wasps' nest is on the trunk of a kauri pine in New Zealand. Like all social wasps' nests, it is made of paper, which is manufactured by the wasps. Some solitary wasps use mud to make their nests. A wasp nest is begun with one group of cells. It is then built on.

Although honey-bees and wasps both form colonies and care for their larvae, they differ from each other in many respects. Honey-bee colonies are permanent; the bees store food during summer to keep them alive during winter. Wasp colonies die at the end of summer. Only the queen survives.

Bees construct their cells of wax, made from pollen collected from flowers, but wasps have no wax glands and so cannot make wax. Instead they use paper, made from wood pulp. They scrape thin slivers of wood from fences and dead trees and chew them up to form a pulp. When the queen awakes in spring she makes the first nest, which is a very small one, usually shaped like an umbrella. The cells, which are also made of paper, are fastened underneath this dome.

Wasps do not feed their larvae on nectar collected from flowers, like bees do. They are carnivorous. The queen wasp feeds on insects and chews some of them into a pulp for feeding the larvae. When the first brood of young wasps emerge they set to work to help the queen enlarge the nest. They build a new and wider layer of cells underneath the first. The queen lays an egg in each cell.

This exotic wasp has made an oddly-shaped nest in a tropical forest. The long stalk is a protection against predators crawling along the branch above. The nest, like those of most wasps, is made of a kind of paper. The wasp uses tiny scraps of wood which she scrapes off with her tongue and she then mixes them with saliva to form the paper. Most wasps' nests have umbrella-like roofs and are entered from underneath.

By the end of the summer a colony of common wasps may consist of as many as 20,000 insects, but other wasps live alone or in only small colonies. Wasps are carnivorous. They feed their larvae on pulped insects.

Bumble-bees form colonies, just as honey-bees and wasps do, but there are only about 100 to 300 in each. In spring, the queen emerges from hibernation and builds a new nest of moss, fine grass and dead leaves, usually in an old mouse-hole. When she lays her first batch of eggs she seals them in a wax cell and sits on them, to keep them warm.

Bumble-bees collect nectar from flowers and store it in a honey-pot of wax, just inside the nest.

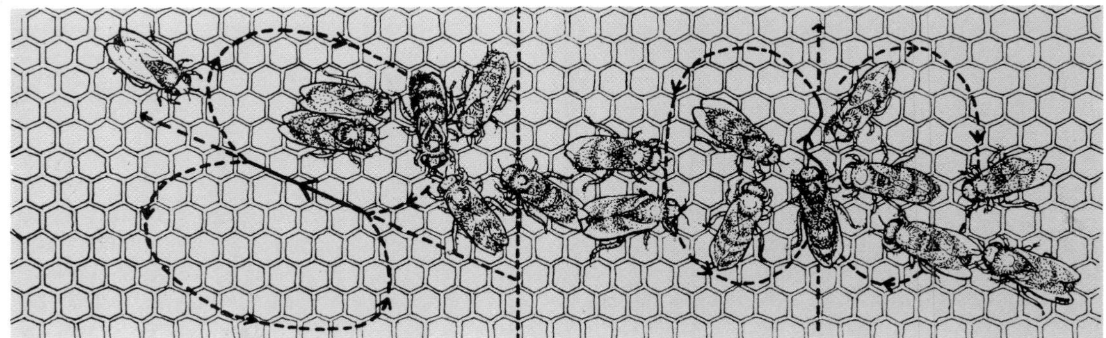

One way in which worker bees communicate ('talk') to each other is by doing a special dance. The dance tells the other bees where to find the flowers which provide them with food. The bee dances in a figure of eight, waggling its body as it dances. A line drawn through the centre of the figure is at the same angle to a line drawn at the vertical, as the angle between the sun and the food. The larger the loops in the figure of eight, the farther away is the new source of food which the dancing bee has found. So the bees know not only which direction to take but how far they have to fly.

Termite tunnels

Queen termite

Workers

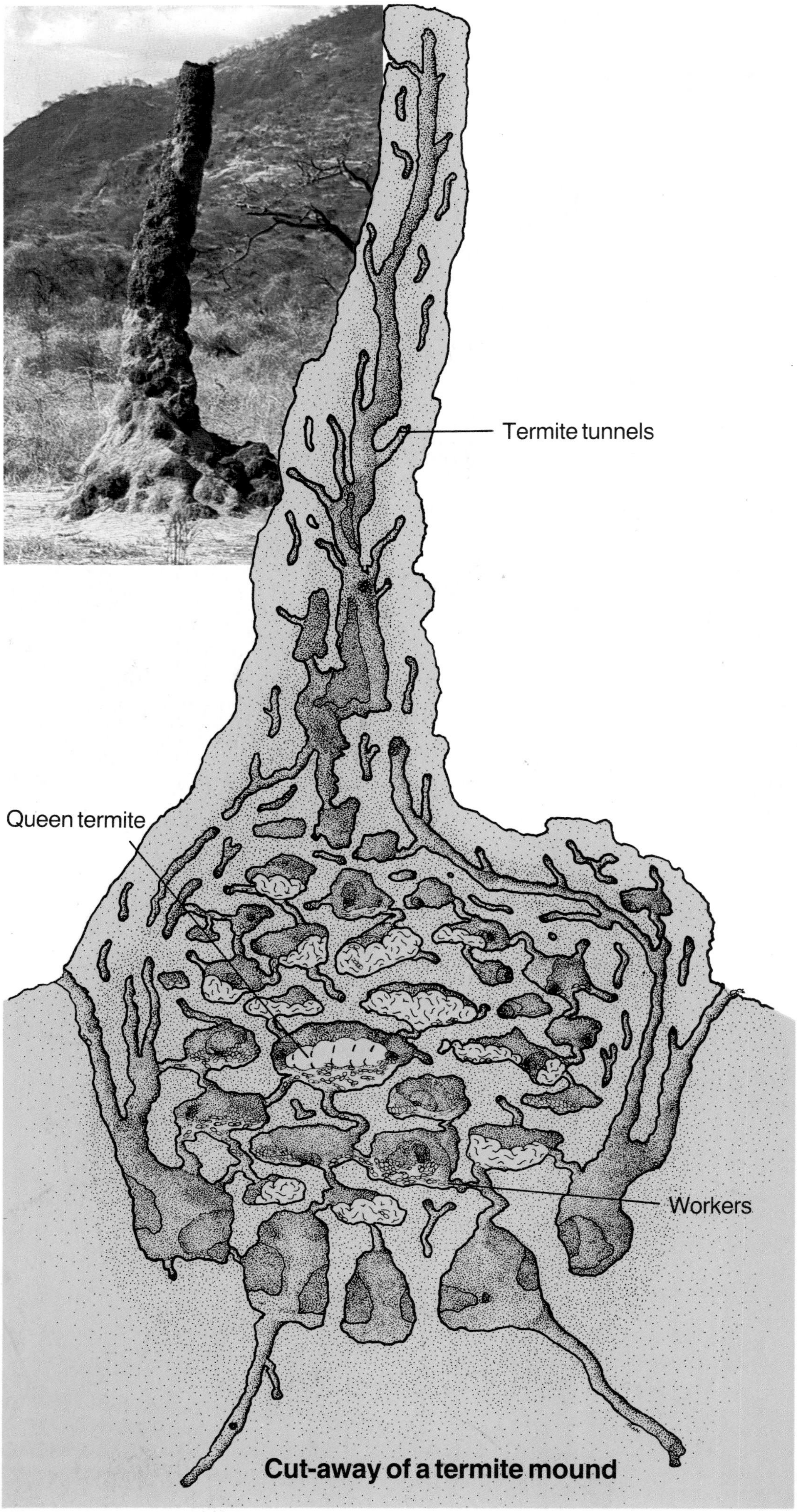

Cut-away of a termite mound

Termite nests are built in many shapes and sizes. This nest in southern Sudan is about seven metres high. It is made from particles of earth fastened together by the termites' saliva, and it is as hard as concrete. In very hot countries some nests are designed so that they have broad surfaces facing the morning and evening sunshine, but a very narrow one facing the midday sun. This arrangement helps to control the temperature inside the nest. Termite nests also extend deep underground. Termites are found mainly in tropical countries, although there are some in Italy and Greece.

Termites are social insects, like bees. As well as making mounds of fantastic shapes, they extend their nests a long way underground. They have a queen to lay eggs, and workers to collect food and attend to the larvae. They also have a king, who helps the queen to dig the first burrow for a new colony. The colonies also have soldiers to defend them. These soldiers have huge heads and jaws, and some of them can squirt a sticky liquid at their enemies. Termite colonies sometimes consist of as many as ten million termites.

The queen termite grows to an enormous size. She looks like a big, fat sausage. She is really not much more than an egg-producing machine. She lays as many as 30,000 eggs a day and may continue to lay eggs for 40 or 50

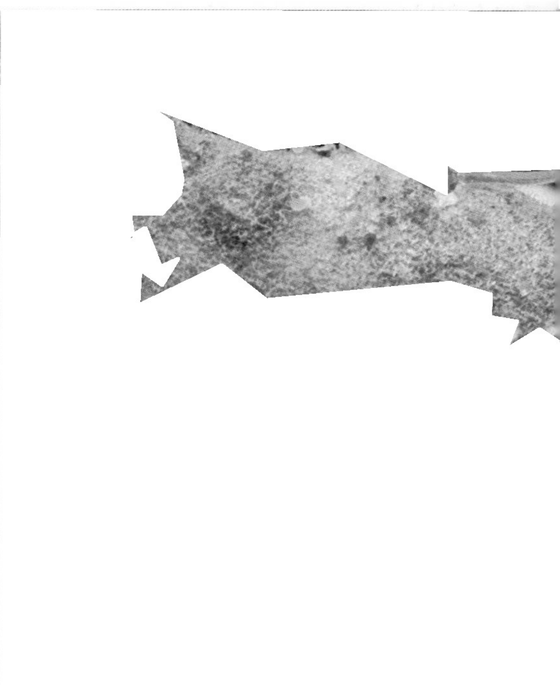

Termites have learned how to grow food. They cultivate fungi on wood pulp so that the termites can eat it. Young termites develop according to the diet they receive. By feeding the larvae

Ants, too, live in colonies with an egg-laying queen, a few males and a host of workers. As with honey-bees the colonies last for several years. Driver ants also have soldiers, which have large, sharp jaws. Sometimes these ants form immense columns which march through the countryside, killing and eating everything they find.

Some kinds of ants keep aphids in their nests or on food-plants nearby. The ants enjoy feeding on the sweet honey-dew which the aphids produce, while the aphids enjoy protection from enemies by the ants.

years. She is active only when she is young and starting to found a colony. When she settles down to produce eggs and has a staff of attendants, the worker termites feed her, groom her and take care of the eggs.

Atta ants also grow fungus. In order to do so they make a compost of green leaves. This compost generates heat. The ants have scissor-like jaws which they use for snipping off pieces of leaves. They carry the leaves back to their nest. These ants are found in immense numbers in the forests of South America. Long columns of them may be seen marching along the forest floor, bearing their leaf segments like banners.

certain foods the workers ensure that the termite colony has the right numbers of soldiers, nurses, general workers and those which do other duties.

Weaving ants make their nests in trees. They fasten leaves together with strands of silk, which are produced by the ant larvae. When weaving, worker ants pass the larvae from one to another, while other workers hold the leaves in place. The ant larvae spin the silk from special glands. These ants live in tropical forests in Australia and South-East Asia.

Locusts and Grasshoppers

Not very many insects can make sounds which we can hear, but grasshoppers and crickets 'sing' all day long in warm, sunny weather. Some of them are noisy at night as well. They make their song by rubbing the inside of a hind-leg against the thick, nobbly vein in a forewing. The warmer the weather, the more vigorously they sing. As the temperature rises, so the number of chirps per second increases. They can hear each other's singing quite well, but their ears are in their legs!

Grasshopper nymphs are very like tiny grasshoppers. They do not go through a pupa stage but split open their skin and cast it away when they grow too big for it. Some crickets do this ten times or more before they become adult.

Grasshoppers feed mostly on plants. In temperate climates they eat grass and other low-growing plants, but many of the tropical grasshoppers feed on leaves. As camouflage, they look very like leaves, even having markings like leaf veins, so that, although they are quite large, they cannot be seen until they move. One of the biggest tropical grasshoppers is 13 centimetres long. It is because grasshoppers and locusts are plant-eaters that they are so greatly feared. Sometimes swarming locusts cover the ground ankle-deep.

Although some crickets are plant-eaters they also eat other insects and animal matter. While grasshoppers and locusts are most active by day, most crickets prefer the evening twilight.

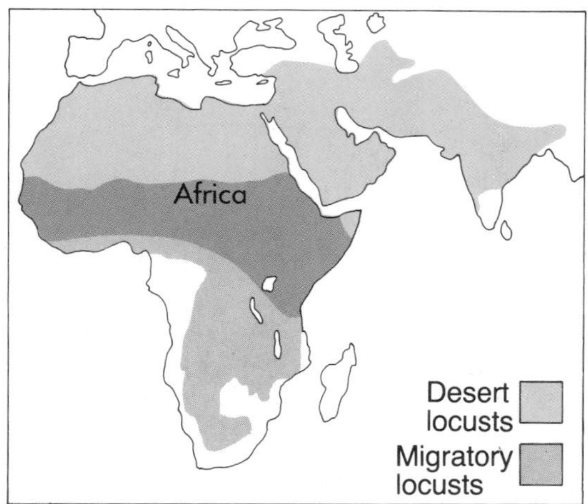

The map shows the areas of Africa and southern Asia where locust swarms occur. There are two common kinds of locusts: the Desert locust and the Migratory locust. Both are found in a wide zone in central Africa, and are carried by the wind when migrating.

This African is walking through a cloud of locusts. There are so many that the sky is darkened. Already they have started to settle and eat the green plants. Soon they will have eaten every leaf and blade of grass and the countryside will be bare. Some locust swarms cover thousands of square kilometres and cause famines in the lands they visit. A swarm once seen crossing the Red Sea was estimated to contain 250,000 million insects.

When locusts breed so rapidly that they use up the local food-supply, they produce a generation different in many ways from their parents. With Desert locusts, for instance, the solitary insects have brown bodies but the swarming ones are yellow with spotted wings. Young locusts, known as hoppers, are green in the solitary phase but become black and yellow for swarming. Swarming locusts have strong wings capable of long flights. The spotted wings show that the locusts in the picture are swarming locusts.

Above: Very long, slender antennae distinguish the Great Green Bush-cricket from other grasshoppers. The long, dangerous-looking 'tail' is not a sting but an ovipositor. The female uses this to make a slit in the soil in which to lay her eggs. Bush-crickets are usually active in the evenings and at night.

Below: This vividly-coloured South African grasshopper is one of nearly 10,000 kinds of grasshopper which have short horns, or antennae. Although grasshoppers move mainly by hopping, many of them can also fly quite well. Their larvae, also known as hoppers like the larvae of locusts, are like the adults but much smaller.

Living in Crowds

There are many groups of insects that live together in large crowds. This can be for a variety of reasons.

Many butterflies lay their eggs in clusters. When the caterpillars hatch they find themselves on a food-plant chosen for them by their mother. They then start to eat the food-plant. For instance you will find the newly-hatched caterpillars of a Large White Butterfly all grouped together on one leaf. A few days later, however, they will disperse all over the plant.

Living in large groups is, for these caterpillars, just a temporary arrangement. They do so only because it is where they happen to be born and it is where their food is. There is, however, some advantage in feeding together. Supposing a hungry bird comes along and you are a caterpillar feeding with ninety-nine other caterpillars. The chances are 100 to 1 against the bird picking you!

Other insects assemble in crowds for other purposes. Mayflies dance in clouds over lakes and ponds when they come together for mating. Locusts assemble in huge numbers for migration. Certain ladybirds and flies cluster together for hibernation.

Social insects, such as bees, ants and wasps, live permanently in crowded colonies. They are called social because they are members of a society. A worker bee or an ant or a queen termite could not live on its own. Each fits into a community where it has specialized work to do. If you took a worker bee and released it miles from its hive, it would soon die. If you took the queen away, all the other bees in the hive would die, unless another queen was hatched quickly. Social insects cannot live without each other.

In a termite colony the queen becomes so dependent on the workers that she cannot move by herself. Her attendants feed her, keep her body damp and clean and care for her eggs. Other workers cultivate fungi in special gardens, for food for the colony. Leaf-cutter ants in South America also cultivate fungi for food, growing them on compost made from leaves which they snip from trees and carry underground.

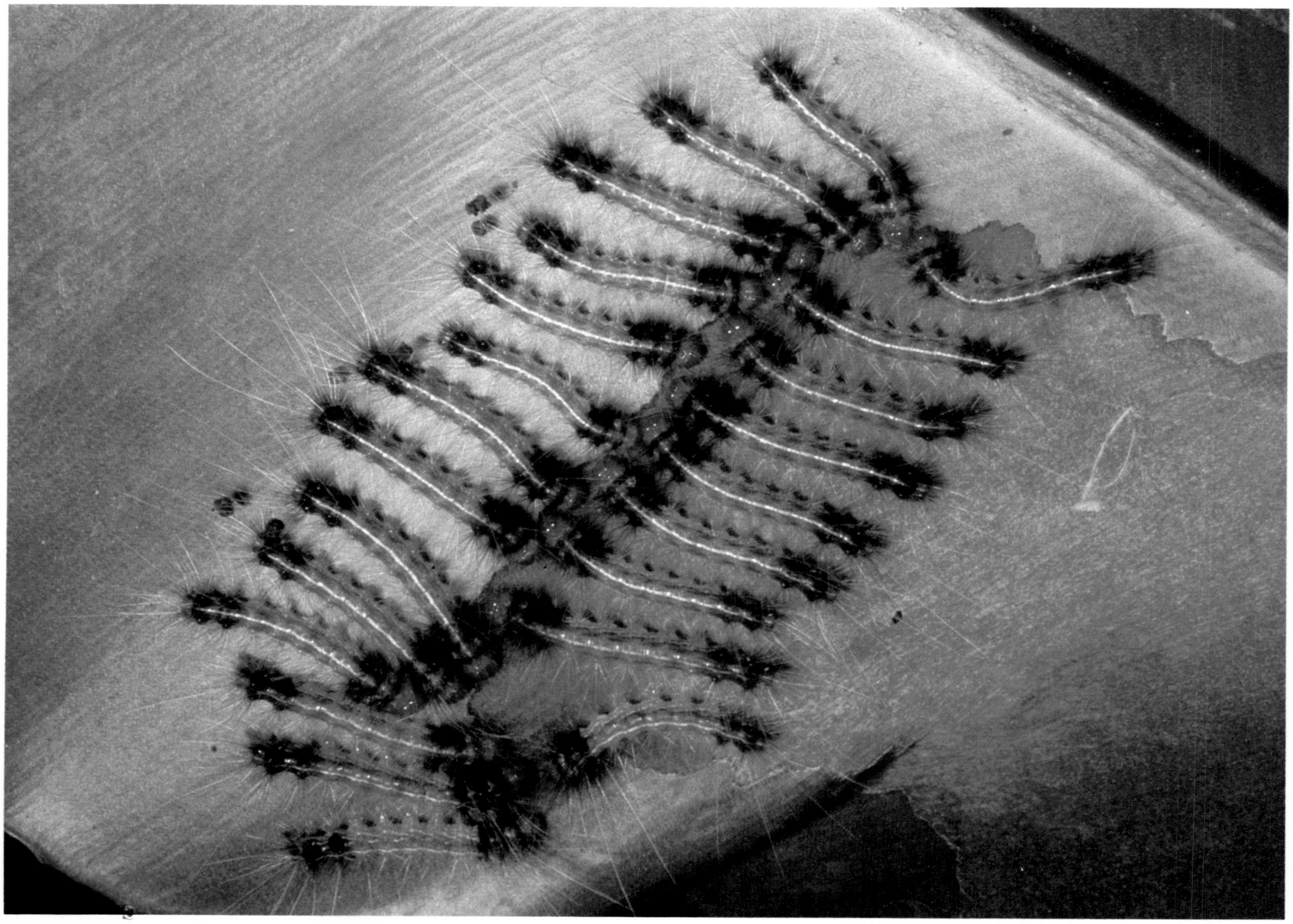

Left: Monarch butterflies migrate in vast numbers. In winter, they breed in Mexico and neighbouring countries. In spring they fly northwards to the United States and Canada. On their journeys, many of them stop to rest on the same tree every year. They crowd together and look like brown leaves. Monarch butterflies are very powerful fliers. Some have even crossed the Atlantic Ocean and have been found in Europe.

When travelling, they are quite noticeable and could easily be caught by birds. However, their bright black-and-red pattern warns that they are not good to eat.

Below: When most insects become dormant for a long period they do so to survive a cold winter. This is called hibernation. In the hot heart of Australia, living creatures are threatened by heat, not cold. So these Bogong moths are sleeping in summer. This is called aestivation. They are doing so in a crowd, in a crevice in a granite rock in the mountains. Their colour and their arrangement in a dense crowd make them look as though they are a part of the rock. In autumn they will stop aestivating and fly off to lower country. Many animals, such as bears and dormice hibernate, but very few aestivate.

Above: Aphids gather together wherever there is plenty of food. The black ants in this picture are also gathering together – to feed on the honey-dew which the aphids produce. They 'milk' the aphids, like farmers milk cows.

Left: These caterpillars are stripping a bird's-nest fern. They have not yet moved away from the leaf on which they hatched, but they will later. Feeding together gives them some protection. There is some safety for them in being in a crowd, particularly if a bird flies past.

The gorgeous colour of butterflies' wings are made up of thousands of tiny scales, which are arranged in overlapping rows. When we touch them, they rub off and look like powder on our fingers. Some colours are caused by certain chemicals, but others are made by reflected light. As the wings move, the light catches the scales at different angles, causing the colours to change. When some tropical butterflies are in the shade of trees, they appear to be deep black. But when they fly into the sunlight, their wings shine with blue, purple and green.

Many butterflies need bright colours to attract mates, but moths, which fly by night or in the twilight, do not. Any vivid colours they have are usually on the underwings, and so are visible only when the moth opens its wings. A night-flying bird chasing a moth is confused when the moth suddenly disappears. All that has happened is that the moth has closed its wings and alighted.

Moths find their mates by scent. The antennae of some male moths are able to pick up the scent of a female at a distance of several miles, especially on a quiet night with no wind. Moths also see a different end of the light spectrum from us – they can see ultra-violet light. Some flowers which appear white to us, gleam with colours that attract the moths.

Butterflies are cold-blooded and need the warmth of the sun. In the early morning, when the sun is low, they tend to be sluggish, and they are most active on a sunny afternoon. Butterflies may appear to be flitting aimlessly about, but their activities always have a purpose. They may be looking for nectar-bearing flowers, or, if they are females, for plants on which to lay their eggs. Or they may be searching for mates, a quest in which their bright colours are very useful.

In the evening, the butterflies retire to rest, often on a twig. In rain-storms they hide under a leaf. In the twilight and at night moths become active (though there are a few moths which fly by day). Their large eyes enable them to see quite well, but to find their favourite flowers or their mates they rely mainly on scent. Some moths also have efficient ears, with which they can hear high-pitched sounds, such as the squeaking of bats.

Some butterflies and moths are camouflaged to make them appear to be dangerous insects. One method is to have markings like large eyes on their wings. When a predator approaches they 'flash' their wings, by opening and shutting them quickly. This startles the enemy into thinking that they are the eyes of a very large animal.

The huge 'eyes' on the wings of the Giant Peacock moth are protective. Its enemies, such as birds, do not attack it because they think they can see the 'eyes' of a large animal. If the moth

The Idea Hypermnestra butterfly of Taiwan, seen here sipping nectar from a flower, is a member of the family to which the Monarch butterfly also belongs. It is also known as the Map butterfly, because its markings resemble those on a map. It is found near water in forest country.

These blue Ithomia butterflies, feeding on birds' droppings in Trinidad, are almost transparent. They have hardly any scales on their wings and are

opens and shuts its wings rapidly it looks as though the eyes are blinking. If the moth closes its wings, the eyes disappear and the bird loses sight of its prey.

therefore very difficult to detect until they fly away. These butterflies feed, sleep and lay their eggs at exactly the same time every day.

The Moon moth of India is one of the largest moths in the world. It has a wing-span of 10 to 12 centimetres. Here seen resting on a tree fern, it is usually seen in the bush growth beneath tropical forests. The antennae of the male are so sensitive that they can detect a female up to eight kilometres away.

The brilliant Salamis butterflies of East Africa seem to disappear the moment they alight. The undersides of the wings are coloured yellowish-brown and have a dark line across them just like the mid-rib of a leaf. In some there are even patches bare of scales, to imitate a hole in the leaf.

Camouflage is disguise. A well-camouflaged creature is one which blends with its surroundings so well that it is very difficult to detect, even when it is out in the open. Some moths, for instance, have markings on their wings that make them look like leaves, tree bark or a flower. It is, of course, necessary for them to remain perfectly still in order to be well camouflaged. Any movement will make them visible again.

When butterflies, moths, grasshoppers, dragonflies and other insects with brightly-coloured wings are in flight, they rely on speed and the ability to dodge for protection against their enemies. But when they alight, they become invisible. So many insects show their vivid colours only when their wings are open. When they are closed they match their surroundings. Most grasshoppers are rather drably coloured in brown and green; but some have striking patterns of red and black visible only when they open their wings.

Camouflage is not only for protection. It is used also by predatory creatures which lie in ambush. The Praying Mantis is one example. It remains motionless, looking like part of a plant, until an unfortunate insect comes within range. Then it seizes the insect in a flash. This mimicry is a very effective form of camouflage.

Even larvae and pupae use camouflage. Most of them fit perfectly into their surroundings. The yellowish cocoons of Burnet moth pupae are of just the same colour as the dead grass stems to which they are fastened. A weevil which feeds on the figwort plants has pupae which look exactly like figwort seeds. Looper caterpillars can easily be mistaken for twigs or leaf stems. They stay quite still when they sense danger. The larvae of Caddis-flies cover themselves with cases of sand, plant material and tiny shells which match the bottom of the streams where they live.

Below: The larvae or nymphs of the Cuckoo-spit insect, or Froghopper, surround themselves with a mass of frothy bubbles. This protects them from birds and also helps to keep their bodies moist. Even rain does not wash away the foam, which often remains long after the insect has gone away.

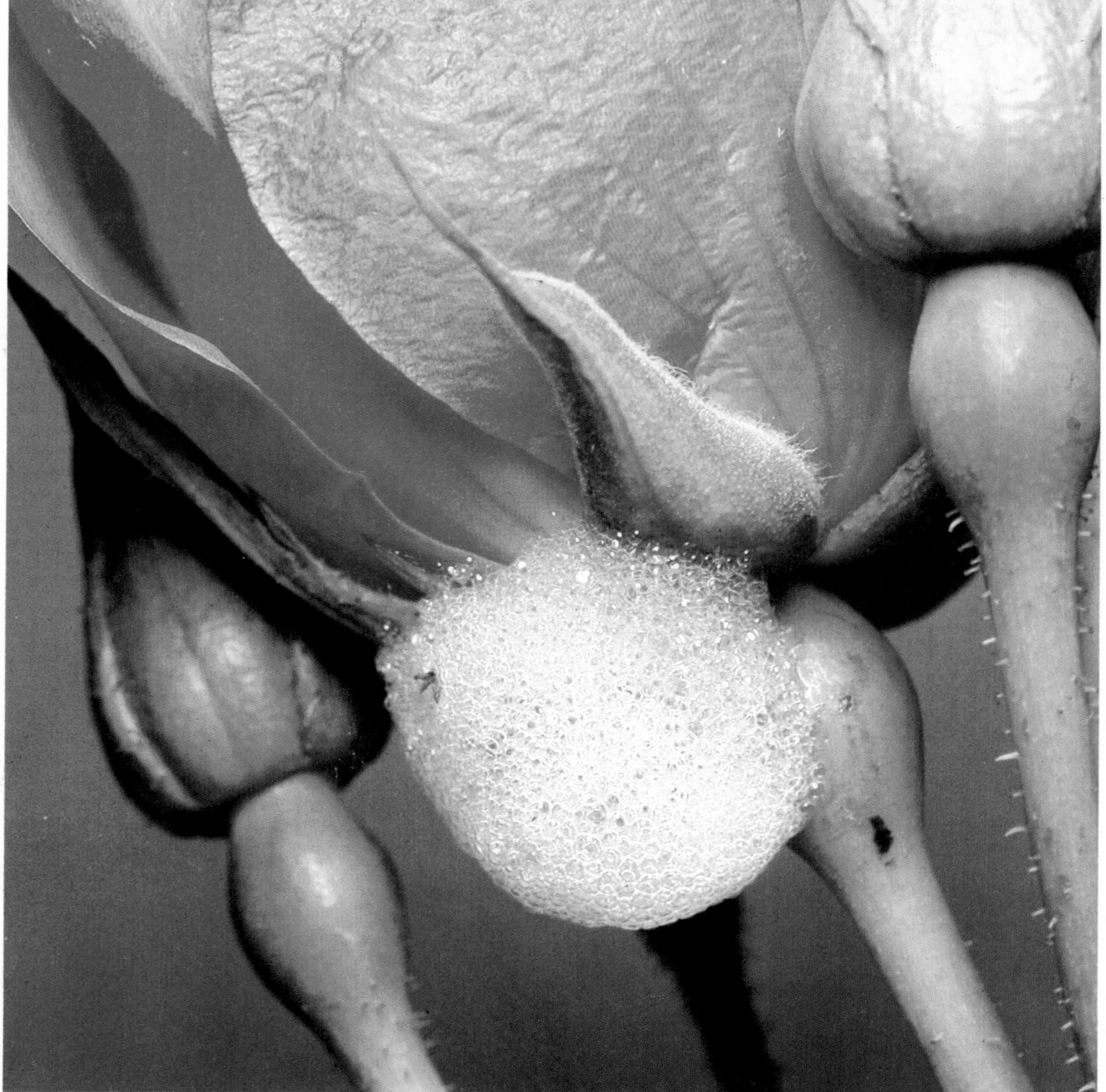

Above: The Lappet moth is a handsome and quite large insect. It has reddish-brown wings patterned with dark, zigzag lines. When it alights on a twig, however, it folds its wings loosely, to resemble a bunch of dead leaves, and seems to disappear completely. Notice how closely the moth in the picture matches the leaves on which it is resting. It even seems to have a stem like theirs.

Above: There are two types of Peppered moths, the light and the dark. Once, most of these moths belonged to the light type. But gradually the dark ones have become much more common, especially in towns. That is because the dark, sooty colour matches the soot-coloured surfaces of tree-trunks and walls in industrial areas.

Right: These Stick insects are long and thin. By day they sit motionless on a twig, stem or blade of grass, moving about only at night to feed. Some Stick insects are flattened and resemble leaves. The females produce eggs quite readily. They can do this without mating, so male Stick-insects are very scarce. The larvae are active little creatures.

Most Stick-insects are tropical and, although the common Stick-insect lives in parts of Europe, it needs to live in warm surroundings. When kept as a pet, it needs to live in a warm room. It will eat the leaves of rose, privet and, if necessary, ivy.

Right: You can hardly see this colony of Thorn-bugs. They look just like real thorns. They will not be noticed until they move. Thorn-bugs are found on thorn trees in tropical regions. They are bright and attractive in colour and very different from the unpleasant, blood-sucking Bed-bugs, though they belong to the same family of insects. Many kinds of bugs like these feed on the juices of plants and are known as plant-bugs. Water scorpions, Back-swimmers and Pond-skaters, which speed about on the surface of ponds, are all kinds of bugs.

Mimicry and Warning Colours

Yellow and black, orange and black, and red and black are warning colours in Nature. When we see a yellow and black insect we fear that it may bite or sting, especially if we have ever been stung by a wasp. Many insects which are quite harmless try to protect themselves by using the same colours.

Creatures, such as birds, animals and predatory insects, learn by experience that certain colours are associated with a nasty taste. Young birds will seize and eat insects like a ladybird or a Soldier-beetle, but only once or twice. They find the taste too unpleasant. And after those early experiments, the birds do not touch either ladybirds or Soldier-beetles, or other insects with similar colouring.

Not all warning colours are a bluff, though. Red ants look dangerous, and so they are. They can squirt formic acid up to 30 centimetres at an enemy.

Some insects change their habits by evolution. This is to make their mimicry more effective. A family of moths known as Clearwings look very like bees and wasps. This protective colouring would not be of much use if they flew by night, like most moths, so they visit flowers by day. They also make a humming noise, like bees, when they fly along.

Below: This Hover-fly is sitting on the flowers of the goldenrod. It looks so like a wasp or a bee, with its pattern of orange and black, that birds are unlikely to touch it. It even has a hairy thorax, like a bee. You can see that it is a fly, however, because it has only two wings, whereas bees and wasps have four.

Bee Hawk-moths emerge from their chrysalids with scales on their wings, but when they start flying, they soon shake them off. Then they look just like Bumble-bees. These moths usually fly only between ten o'clock and midday on sunny mornings.

The mimicry of the Clearwing moths is designed to deceive birds which might otherwise prey on them. Some other insects use mimicry to deceive the insects which they are copying. For instance, there is a certain fly which looks and behaves like a Bumble-bee. It even buzzes like one. It feeds on the rubbish in Bumble-bees' nests, including dead larvae. It is a sort of scavenger. The Bumble-bees do not notice that it is not one of them, and so they let the fly into the nest.

There is even a male moth which gains protection by mimicking the female. It is the Yellowtail. Both male and female have a tuft of yellow hairs on the tail. The hairs on the female cause intense irritation to any other creature which touches them, and the female gives warning of the danger by flaunting her yellow tail when an enemy approaches. So does the male, but his tail is quite harmless. But the enemy cannot tell the difference, so it leaves them both alone.

Left: These Cinnabar moth caterpillars, feeding on ragwort, have no need to hide themselves. They are protected by their yellow-and-black pattern, which warns predators that they are not good to eat. They have a very unpleasant taste, as young birds quickly discover when they try to eat one.

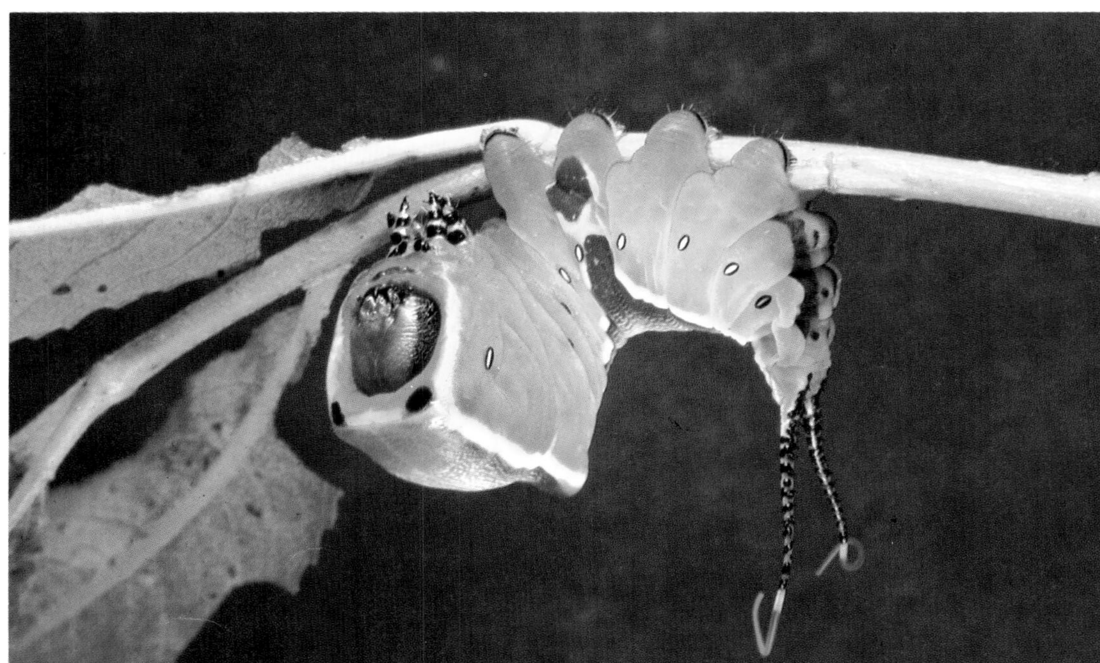

Above: The big, gaudy Foaming Bush-cricket, with its pink and purple colouring, looks as though it might be an unpleasant insect, and so it is. When it is touched or handled it produces a burning and nasty-tasting foam. So it has several ways of protecting itself, for it can leap and fly, like other grasshoppers and crickets.

Left: When the Puss moth caterpillar is disturbed, it rears up to show a frightening mask to its attacker. At the same time, it lashes out with its two red tail-threads. In addition, it can squirt out a jet of stinging acid if its attacker does not go away. When the caterpillar is feeding, the brightly-coloured mask and the red tail-threads are hidden.

Dragonflies, Beetles and Others

Beetles are the most numerous of all the insects. There are more than 300,000 known kinds of them in the world. They range in size from tiny weevils to the giant Goliath-beetles of Africa which are more than 15 centimetres long.

Most beetles can fly, but when they are not flying their gauzy wings are folded up and protected by horny sheaths called 'elytra'. In many beetles the elytra are glossy black but in others they are vividly coloured.

Plant-bugs are also very numerous. This group of insects includes Bed-bugs, aphids, Water-boatmen, Pond-skaters, Froghoppers and Cicadas. They all have beaked mouths, made for piercing and sucking.

Dragonflies are among the largest and most beautiful of insects, but young dragonflies, which are known as nymphs and which live under water, are ugly monsters and very ferocious.

Below: Dragonflies generally rest with their wings spread, displaying their resplendent colours. For safety from enemies, they rely on their eyes, some of which have 20,000 or 30,000 lenses.

Above: Glow-worms are really beetles. The last three segments of the soft body of the female glow-worm glow in the dark with a soft, golden-green light. Its purpose is to attract males, which can fly well and have sharp eyes. The females do not fly and have not very good eyesight. They simply sit on a grassy bank and glow. Glow-worm larvae are fierce little creatures which eat snails.

Above: The Lantern-fly is a plant-bug which sucks sap from trees and other plants. It often does much damage to food crops. The purpose of the curious growth on the front of its head is not known.

Below: Many large and gorgeously-coloured beetles, like this Gold Bug from Ecuador, are found in the tropics. The armour-like covering of their wing-cases and bodies are protection against predators. Indians make ornaments from the shells of the Gold Bugs.

This Lycid beetle, from South Africa, with its strange, flattened wing-cases, feeds on plant tissues. It lays its eggs on the debris beneath plants, and when they emerge the larvae feed on scraps of vegetable matter.

Giants and Monsters

Because of the way in which their bodies are made, insects cannot grow to immense sizes. That is just as well for us. A world in which wasps were as big as vultures and fleas as big as rabbits would be a dangerous place.

The biggest and heaviest insects are Goliath-beetles and certain other tropical insects, which measure over 14 centimetres in length and about 10 centimetres in width, and which weigh almost 100 grams. There are tropical Stick-insects which are much longer (up to 30 centimetres) but not nearly as heavy.

Some Birdwing butterflies of the Solomon Islands have wing-spans of more than 30 centimetres, and several tropical moths measure over 25 centimetres. But butterflies and moths are much lighter in weight than beetles. Giant cockroaches, which sometimes cause alarm because they run so fast, reach lengths of more than eight centimetres. In Indonesia there lives a dragonfly which is more than ten centimetres long and has a wing-span of 20 centimetres.

This picture is a full-face portrait of what appears to be a space-monster. Note the huge, glaring eyes, the sharp-edged lips, and things which look like mechanical arms or legs. The creature is, in fact, a Harlequin beetle, from South America. It measures about eight centimetres long and lives in forests and orchards. Although only the base of them can be seen, the antennae are very long – about 12 centimetres. As it is a night creature it uses them to find its way about the forest. It runs over the forest floor, tapping things with its antennae. Long-horned beetles are wood-borers.

Some insects have the appearance of monsters when seen through a magnifying-glass. The nymphs of dragonflies are horrific creatures, with sharp fangs and hairy legs. The larvae of the Great Diving-beetle, which also live in water, look and are equally fierce. The adult beetle, though much more handsome, is equally bloodthirsty. Some of the ferocious Driver ants of Africa are 3.3 centimetres long.

Some of these ants have developed very large and dangerous-looking jaws. The big 'horns' of male Stag-beetles are, however, controlled by weak muscles and are harmless.

Some of the common flies look repulsive under a magnifying-glass. They have hairy legs, bloated bodies and a fearsome armoury of tools for biting or piercing skin and sucking blood. Their larvae are ugly white maggots. Fleas, lice, bed-bugs and mosquitoes also strike us as being most unattractive; but perhaps that is because we know about their unpleasant habits.

Left: Weevils are distinguished by their long, beak-like snouts and by their four-jointed feet. Most of them are small, but this larger one from tropical rain-forests measures about four centimetres. There are more than 40,000 different kinds of weevils in the world, and some of them are extremely numerous. Some are destructive pests. Nutweevils lay their eggs in the shells of unripe hazelnuts. The larvae eat the kernel as it ripens.

Above: The Ghost-walker, which lives in the forests of Sumatra, is a ground beetle, although this one is clinging to a dead tree-trunk. Its colour and shape make it almost invisible at night, when it is most active. It measures about six centimetres and has curiously flattened body and wing-cases.

Like most beetles, it can fly quite well. Beetles have their forewings adapted to shield their hind-wings.

Left: Rhinoceros beetles, of which there are many kinds, are among the world's largest insects. The largest of all is the Hercules beetle, which grows to a length of 18 centimetres and can weigh up to 100 grams. The males have curious double horns, the purpose of which is unknown. The muscles that control the horns are not very strong. Perhaps the horns are just for ornament, to attract the females. Most Rhinoceros beetles live in tropical forests.

Insects with Strange Homes

Insects are found almost everywhere, even in frozen Antarctica, within 1,400 kilometres of the South Pole. These are tiny insects known as Springtails, which are the commonest insects in the world. There are enormous numbers in every spadeful of garden soil. Bird lice live among the feathers of birds and feed on particles of feather and skin. Book lice live in libraries, eating the paste of the book bindings. Almost every vertebrate has an insect parasite.

If we handle a young house-martin or swallow straight from the nest we shall find in their feathers some horrid little crab-like creatures with clinging feet. These are louse-flies, which are wingless. Many of them spend the winter in the old nests of the birds and are there waiting for them when they return in spring. Other wingless flies of the same family attack sheep, deer, horses and bats.

Many insects spin cocoons of silk in which to live. Commercial silk, which was in common use before nylon was invented, is made by the larvae of Silk moths. The larvae of Caddis-flies use silk to bind together scraps of leaves and stones to form a protective case for their soft bodies. Ant-lions, which are the larvae of a fly, live in the sand at the bottom of a pit, waiting for ants to fall in so they can eat them.

Above: These galls on a tree leaf are the homes of larvae of a Gall-wasp. There is one larva in each gall. When the leaves begin to wither in autumn, the galls fall off and are buried in the debris beneath the tree. There the larvae continue to grow for a time. Later they pupate, and the mature Gall-wasps emerge in spring. There are many other kinds of galls, including Oak-apple and Marble-galls.

When Burying-beetles find the carcase of an animal or bird, they scrape away the soil beneath it until it sinks into the ground. Then the female lays her eggs in a little tunnel near the corpse, which provides an ideal home and food for her larvae. She remains on guard until the eggs hatch.

When the Large Blue butterfly caterpillar is first hatched, it feeds on wild thyme. Then it starts to wander, and ants find it and carry it to their

Right: The curious patterns on this bramble leaf are made by the larvae of a moth. They live between the upper and lower surfaces of the leaf and are called Leaf-miners.

underground nest because they like to lick the honey-dew which the caterpillar produces. In the nest the caterpillar feeds on ant larvae.

The Scarab, or Dung-beetle, rolls the dung of a plant-eating animal into a ball and then lays its eggs in it. When the larva hatches, it feeds on the dung, while the female beetle stays on guard over this strange home. Other Dung-beetles roll balls of dung into underground stores for their larvae to feed on.

Enemies of Man

Although insects are so small, those which are enemies of human beings are very formidable. They are dangerous in three ways.

Some are our competitiors, eating or damaging the food we want for ourselves. Maggots in apples and wasps eating plums are examples. It has been estimated that from ten to 30 per cent of all cultivated crops are destroyed by insects.

Some insects are parasites, such as fleas, lice and Bed-bugs. These were once common everywhere, and although their numbers have been reduced in many western countries they have not been exterminated.

Some insects are carriers of disease germs. Mosquitoes are amongst the most dangerous enemies of human beings. They not only suck human blood but carry such deadly diseases as malaria and yellow fever. Common house-flies can carry typhoid, cholera and dysentery.

Above: Although the Grain weevil is very small, it is a serious pest where grain is stored. It lays its eggs in the grain, which the larvae eat from inside. In the picture, you can see some of the empty husks, and some with the larvae still inside. Grain weevils and their larvae thrive best in warm, damp conditions. They need a temperature of at least 18°C to breed. So farmers and millers try to dry their grain thoroughly and store it at a low temperature.

Left: The caterpillars of the Large White butterfly are a common pest in the garden. Here, a colony is feeding on a cabbage leaf. When the caterpillars are small they feed close together. They keep in contact with each other by means of scent. As they grow bigger they disperse to every part of the leaf. They will eat every part of it except the larger ribs. Their colour pattern of yellow and black warns birds that they are unpleasant to eat.

Right: Colorado potato beetles used to live only in parts of western America. Now, they have spread to most countries where potatoes are grown. They cause enormous damage by feeding on the leaves. Millions can be found in an infested potato-field. The adults have black-and-yellow stripes, and the pink larvae have black spots. During summer, the larvae turn into orange-coloured pupae. The adult beetles emerge in autumn but hibernate underground.

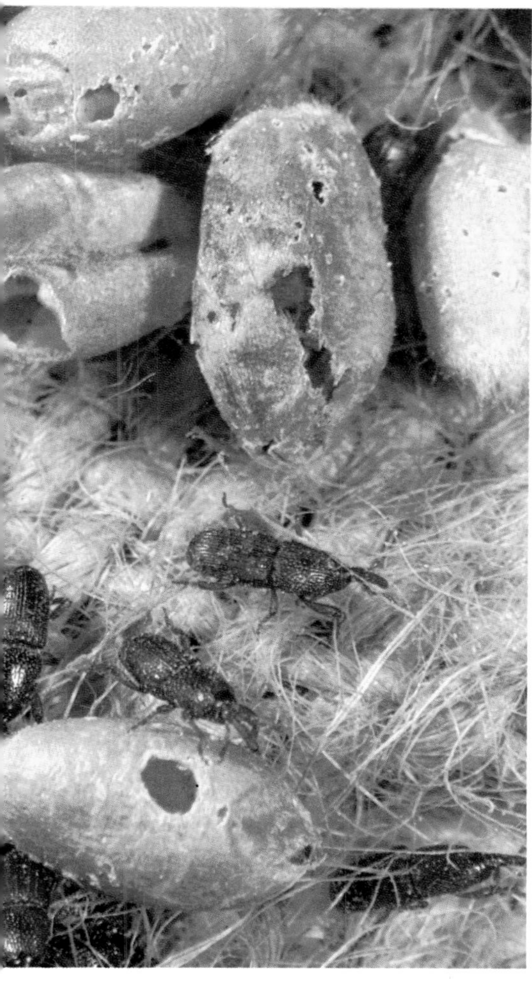

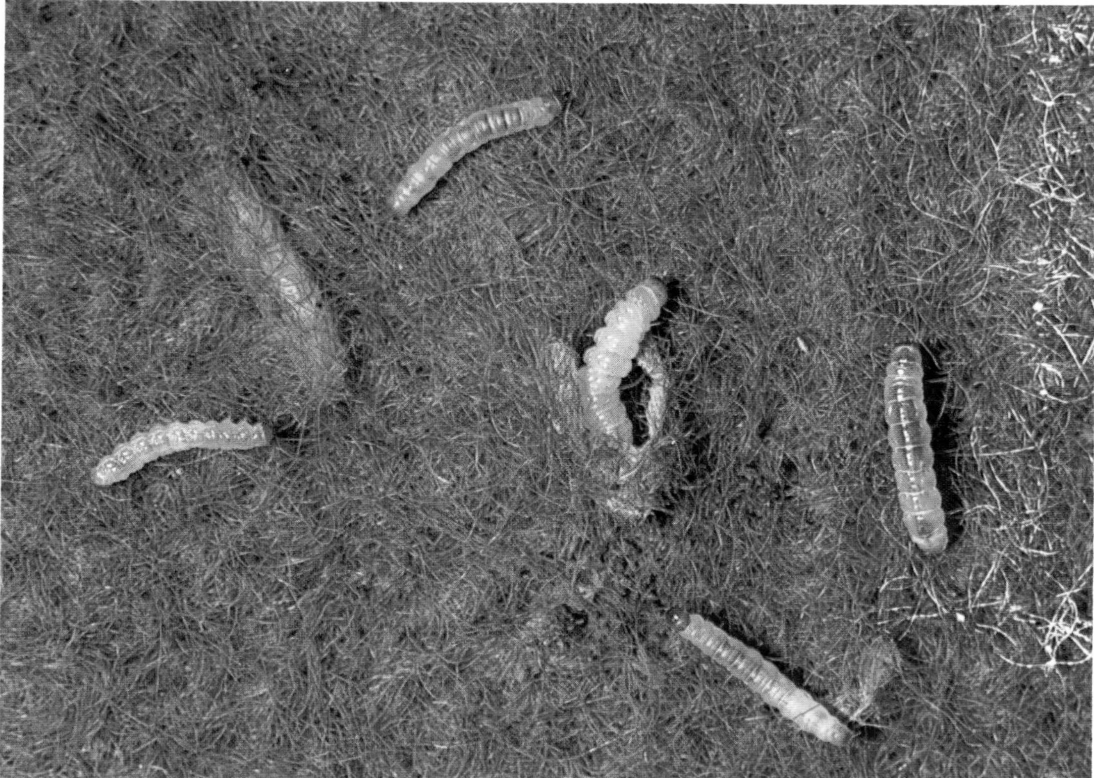

These larvae of the Brown House-moth are feeding on a carpet underspread. They will eat anything made of wool, fur or similar material, and can do quite a lot of damage. The moths fly in summer. Before these moths found an unlimited supply of fabrics for their larvae to eat in the homes of men, they lived in birds' nests, where there were plenty of feathers and rubbish for food.

We can easily see the damage that caterpillars are doing to our cabbages or aphids to our roses. But other larvae may be eating the roots of our cultivated plants; and we do not notice what is happening until the plants start to wilt and die. Competitive insects are so dangerous because they are so numerous. Many thousands of people in tropical countries have starved because vast swarms of locusts have eaten their food crops.

One of the most effective methods of controlling pests is to use pesticides. These are poisonous chemicals which are sprayed over gardens and fields. They are usually very effective, but they kill other insects as well as the pests. And after a time the pests breed generations which are immune to the poison. Scientists then have to discover another chemical, and so the endless war goes on.

Another popular method of controlling pests is to use parasitic or predatory insects. For instance, ladybirds eat aphids. When the numbers of aphids increase, so do the numbers of ladybirds. In California a plant-bug which was playing havoc with the orange orchards was controlled by introducing a beetle which fed on it.

Many aquatic insects spend only the larval or nymphal stage of their lives under water. Dragonfly nymphs live entirely in the water and breathe through gills, but when they are ready to become adults they climb up a plant stalk, split their skins and fly away.

There are even some moths whose caterpillars have gills and live entirely under water. They make for themselves cases formed from the submerged leaves of water-plants bound together by silk. In due course they change into pupae inside the cases. When they emerge, the moths crawl to the surface and fly.

Other aquatic insects do not have gills and so need to come to the surface from time to time, to breathe air. Some of them keep the greater part of their bodies under water, with just a breathing-tube projecting above the surface.

Other insects live on, rather than under, the water. Pond-skaters skim over the surface on specially padded feet. Water-gnats actually crawl on the water.

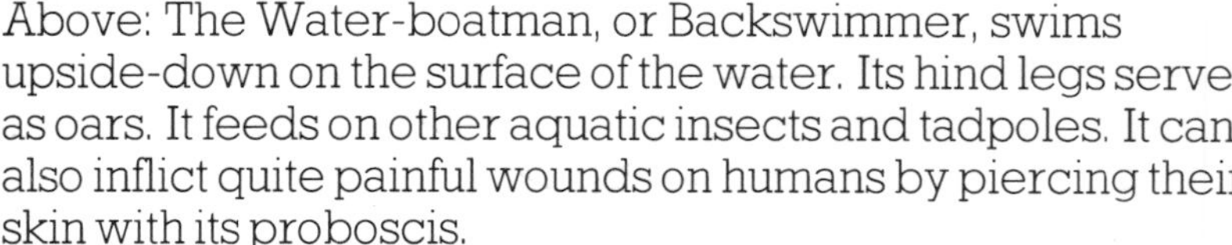

Above: The Water-boatman, or Backswimmer, swims upside-down on the surface of the water. Its hind legs serve as oars. It feeds on other aquatic insects and tadpoles. It can also inflict quite painful wounds on humans by piercing their skin with its proboscis.

Above: The Great Diving-beetle, or Great Water-beetle, is one of the largest British beetles, measuring up to 3.5 centimetres in length. Its hind legs are flattened to form oars, which it uses just like a human rower would use oars. Although it spends most of its time in the water, it can fly well and often finds its way to isolated ponds and water-troughs. It is a fierce insect, preying on other insects, tadpoles and small fish. It will even kill and eat goldfish in a garden pond. The larvae, which grow to a length of five centimetres, are equally aggressive. They fasten their jaws on their victim and suck it dry. The larvae are lighter than water and stay underwater by clinging on to weeds.

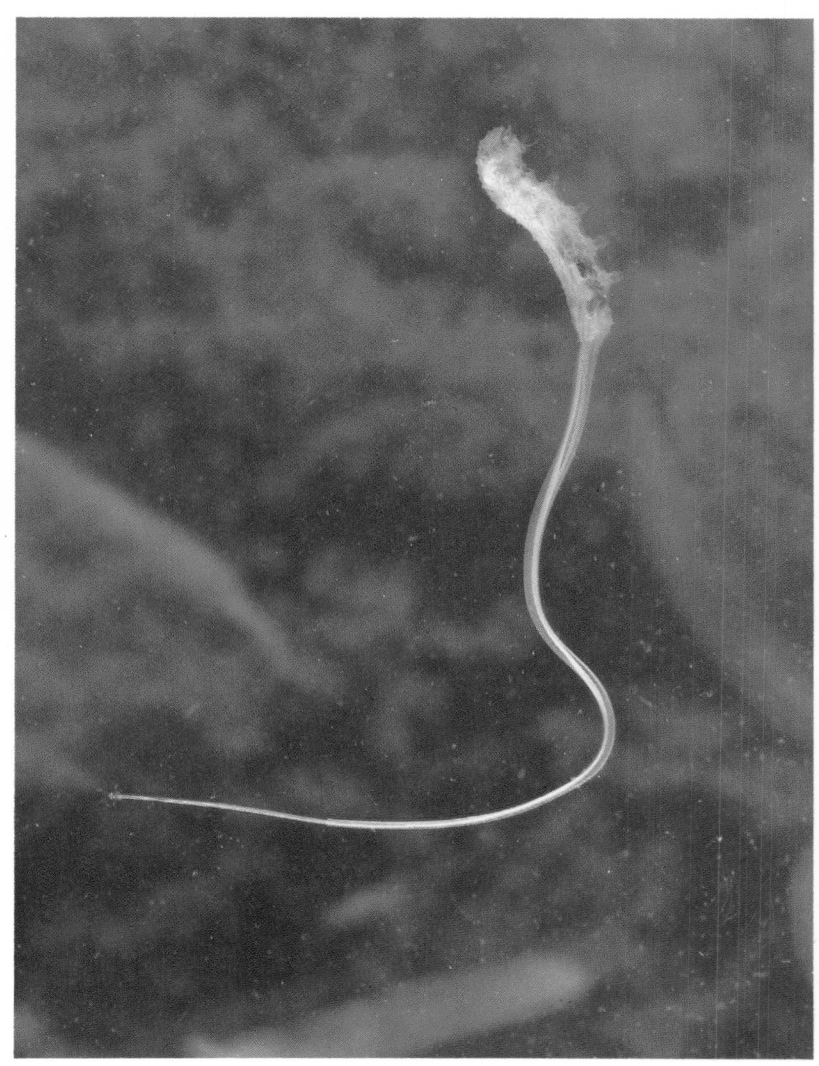

Left: The Rat-tailed maggot is the larva of a Hover-fly, commonly known as the Drone-fly. It sits on the bottom of muddy ponds and breathes through its long tail, the tip of which shows just above the water. While its tail-end is breathing, its front end is searching for scraps of plant and animal matter in the mud. The breathing-tube can be made longer or shorter, according to the depth of the water. The pupa floats just under the surface of the water.

Above: Caddis-fly larvae protect their soft bodies by surrounding them with cases of sticks, stones, leaves and shells, fastened together by silk. These larvae in a river in Hampshire, England, are able to move about freely. However, some other kinds anchor themselves to weeds. Adult Caddis-flies fly mostly at dusk. Fish and water-birds love to eat Caddis-worms, but one kind of larva outwits them by fixing twigs that are too big to swallow to its case.

Large Mexican Grasshopper

Most grasshoppers are protected by their colouring, which is usually in patterns of green and brown, to match the plants on which they feed. They also have very powerful hind legs, which enable them to leap away from danger. Many of them can fly as well. This Mexican grasshopper, when resting on a leaf or blade of grass, is green and yellow. But when it spreads its wings, it shows a pattern of red and black.

Observing Insects and Glossary

You will now want to find out more about insects for yourself. The main problem is that there are so many insects you could study that it is hard to know where to begin. Perhaps it is best to start with some of the biggest and most easily seen insects, such as caterpillars.

A useful caterpillar cage is a box with a panel of perforated zinc on one side or in the lid. Cover the floor of the box with soil and, if possible, put a layer of peat moss litter over the soil. Supply the caterpillars with fresh food each day, standing the plant-stems in a little jar of water to keep them fresh. Most caterpillars will feed by night, hiding under the leaves by day. They grow very quickly and cast their skins several times as they grow. After a few weeks they will be ready to pupate. Some will want to bury themselves in the soil at the bottom of the cage. Others will spin a cocoon and suspend themselves from the side of the cage or from the food-plant. Caterpillars found in autumn will spend the winter as chrysalids, but those found in spring may emerge as adult insects within a few weeks.

Or you may want to keep aquatic insects. For these you will need a glass tank or aquarium, complete with a good growth of pondweed. Insects you can keep there include the larvae of dragonflies and water-beetles. Remember that both are very fierce, carnivorous creatures. They will eat any other insects they can catch, even each other. You will have to keep them well fed on small earth-worms and flies. Adult water-beetles are interesting insects to have in an aquarium, and one species, the Silver water-beetle, feeds on decaying vegetable matter. A soft lettuce leaf rotting on the surface of the water will suit it nicely. Remember, though, that adult water-beetles can fly well, so cover your aquarium if you want to keep them.

A glass tank can also be used as a formicarium, which is a place where ants are kept. An ants' nest, complete with inmates, should be lifted as carefully as possible and put in the tank, with plenty of additional soil or leaf debris for the ants to work with. With luck, the ants will build their nest with a cross-section against the glass, so you will be able to watch what they are up to.

Another insect which lives in communities is, of course, the honey-bee, and you may be attracted to the idea of possessing a bee-hive. This is much more complicated and you must get professional advice and wear protective clothing. You can have a glass panel fitted over the frames of comb, so that you can see what the bees are doing.

Glossary

Aestivation	The habit of spending very hot summers asleep or dormant.
Antenna	A feeler; the organ attached to the head of some insects.
Aphis	A small soft-bodied insect which sucks the juices of plants.
Camouflage	Hiding by means of disguise.
Chitin	A hard, horny substance forming the casing of the bodies of many insects.
Chrysalis	The pupa of a butterfly or moth; the third stage of an insect's life.
Cocoon	A silky case covering and protecting a chrysalis.
Elytra	The hard outer wing-cases of beetles.
Hibernation	The habit of spending the winter asleep or dormant.
Larva	The second stage of an insect's life.
Metamorphosis	A change of form, for example from a larva to a pupa.
Mimicry	Imitating another creature in order to gain protection or concealment.
Moulting	Shedding a skin that has become too small.
Nectar	A sweet substance found in flowers and much loved by many insects.
Nymph	The immature form of certain insects, such as dragonflies.
Parasite	A creature that lives on another.
Parthenogenesis	The ability of the females of certain kinds of insects to produce fertile eggs or young without mating.
Pesticides	Chemicals for killing insect pests.
Pollen	The grains of a yellowish substance found in male flowers and necessary for fertilizing female flowers.
Predator	A creature which preys on other creatures.
Proboscis	The snout-like mouth-part of some insects, designed for sucking plant or animal juices.
Pupa	The third state in the life of an insect.
Spiracles	Small holes in its body through which an insect breathes.
Thorax	The chest, or middle part of an insect's body.
Trachea	A passage through which air is conveyed to various parts of an insect's body.

Bee-keeping can be fascinating work, but you have to be very careful. Note that this man is wearing protective clothing, hat and mask so that he does not get stung.

Index

Aestivation 29, 48
Antennae 9, 11, 30-31, 38, 43, 48
Ant-lions 40
Ants 4, 11, 25, 28-29, 34, 39-41, 48
Aphids 8, 10-11, 15, 18-20, 25, 29, 43, 48
Atta ants 25

Back-swimmers 33
Bed-bugs 33, 36, 39, 42
Bee Hawk-moths 35
Bee-keeping 48
Beetles 4, 9-10, 16, 18, 20, 36-38
Bees 4, 6-7, 11, 18-20, 22-25, 28, 48
Birdwing butterflies 38
Black Death, the 7
Blow-flies 6, 14-17
Bogong moths 29
Brown House-moths 43
Bumble-bees 23, 35
Butterflies 4, 7-9, 12-16, 18-19, 28-32, 34, 38

Caddis-flies 32, 40, 45
Caddis-worms 45
Camouflage 7, 12-13, 20-21, 26, 30, 32-33, 48
Carniverous insects 7-8, 12, 15, 20-21, 23, 25, 30, 34, 36-37, 43-44
Caterpillars 4, 8, 10, 12-17, 28-29, 32, 34-35, 40-44, 48
Chalcid wasps 8
Chitin 8, 48
Chrysalids 4, 8, 10-13, 15-16, 35, 48
Cinnabar moths 34-35
Clearwing moths 34-35
Cockroaches 38
Cocoons 10-11, 17, 30, 40, 48
Colonies 7, 17, 22-25, 28-29
Colorado beetles 10, 42-43
Crickets 21, 26-27, 35-36

Deer flies 8
Desert locusts 26
Disease germs 4, 6-7, 15-16, 20, 42
Dragonflies 2-5, 7, 12, 20, 32, 36-39, 44, 48
Driver ants 25, 39

Eggs 10-16, 19, 22-25, 30-31, 33, 37, 40, 42
Elm-bark beetles 16
Emperor moths 14

Fertilization 6-7, 18
Fleas 4, 7, 38-39, 42
Flies 6, 8, 10-11, 14-17, 20, 28, 32, 34, 37, 39, 40, 42, 44
Foaming Bush-cricket 35
Froghoppers 32, 36
Fungi cultivation 4, 24-25, 28

Galls 17, 40-41
Gall-wasps 17, 40-41
Ghost-walker 39
Giant Peacock moths 30-31
Glow-worms 36
Gnats 10-11
Gold Bugs 37
Golden-ringed dragonfly 2-3
Goliath-beetles 36, 38
Grain-weevils 42
Grasshoppers 6, 26-27, 32, 35, 46-47
Great Diving-beetles 39, 44
Great Green Bush-crickets 27
Greenbottle flies 15-16
Ground-beetles 20

Harlequin beetles 38
Hawker dragonflies 4-5
Hercules beetles 39
Hibernation 12, 23, 29, 48
Honey-bees 6-7, 18-19, 20, 22-23, 25, 48
Hoppers 26-27
Horse-flies 8, 20
Hover-flies 34, 44

Ichneumon flies 16
Idea Hypermnestra butterflies 31
Ithomia butterflies 30-31

Lacewings 15
Ladybirds 8, 20, 28, 34, 43
Lantern-flies 37
Lappet moths 32-33
Large Blue butterflies 40-41
Large White butterflies 4, 28, 42, 48
Larvae 4, 6, 8, 10-11, 14-20, 22-25, 27, 30, 32-33, 35-36, 39-45, 48
Leaf-cutter ants 28
Leaf-miners 41
Lice 39-40, 42
Locusts 4, 6, 8, 26-28, 43
Long-horned beetles 38
Looper caterpillars 32
Louse-flies 40
Luna moths 11
Lycid beetles 37

Maggots 15-16, 42, 44
Mating 10-11, 16, 19-20, 22-23, 28, 33
Mayflies 4, 10-11, 19, 28
Mexican grasshoppers 46-47
Migratory locusts 26
Mimicry 20-21, 30-31, 34-35, 48
Monarch butterflies 15, 18-19, 28-29
Moon moths 31
Mosquitos 14-15, 42
Moths 4, 11-12, 14-17, 29-35, 38, 40-41, 43
Moulting 8, 12, 16-17, 44, 48
Mouth-parts 4, 8, 19, 20

Nectar 6-8, 18-20, 22-23, 30-31, 48
Nests 22-25
Nymphs 2-3, 7, 12, 20, 26, 32, 36-37, 39, 44, 48

Pale Tussock moths 16-17
Paradise Swallowtail 7
Parthenogenesis 10-11, 48
Peacock butterflies 12-13, 48
Peppered moths 33
Pesticides 8, 43, 48
Plant-bugs 14, 33, 36
Pollen 6, 18-19, 22, 48
Pond-skaters 33, 36, 44
Praying Mantids 20-21, 32
Privet Hawk-moths 15
Pupae 10-14, 16-17, 26, 30, 32, 44, 48
Puss moths 35

Rag-tailed maggots 44
Rhinoceros beetles 39
Robber-flies 20
Rose aphids 19
Royal jelly 22, 48

Scarab beetles 11, 41
Scent 4, 9, 11, 30, 42
Sense organs 8-9, 14, 16-17, 30, 36
Sexton beetles 16-17
Silk moths 10, 40
'Singing' 6, 26-27
Small Ermine moth 17
Small Tortoiseshell butterflies 48
Small White butterflies 48
Social insects 7, 14, 22-25, 28-29, 48
Soldier-beetles 18, 34
Spiracles 8, 15, 48
Springtails 4, 40
Stag beetles 39
Stick insects 33, 38
Stings 11, 34
Swarms 7, 26-27

Termites 4, 11, 24-25, 28
Thorax 8, 14, 34, 48

Warning colours 18-19, 28, 34-35, 42
Wasps 4, 8, 10-11, 16-17, 22-23, 28, 34, 38
Water-beetles 46, 48
Water-boatmen 36, 44
Water-gnats 44
Water scorpions 33
Weaving ants 25
Weevils 32, 36, 38-39, 42
White flies 8
Wings 4, 8-11, 14-15, 18-20, 26, 30-31, 34, 36, 38-39
Wood-wasps 10-11

Yellowtail moths 35